# In Love And College

## A Practical Guide To Practical Relationships

Stephen C. Phillips

*In Love And College: A Practical Guide To Practical Relationships*

Publisher: ILC Press
Baton Rouge, Louisiana

Cover photo credit: "steenface!" on Flickr. View her photography at www.flickr.com/photos/xtinemarie.

Cover design credit: John Saltiel

ISBN: 978-0-6151-9982-5

Printed in the United States of America.

In all examples and letters, names and other revealing but impertinent details have been changed or omitted to protect the innocent. All letters have also been edited for spelling, grammar, and style.

For free information supplementary to this book, visit www.InLoveAndCollege.com.

"I always pass on good advice. It's the only thing to do with it. It is never any use to oneself."

- Oscar Wilde, *An Ideal Husband*

For Jenna, my bride

# Contents

# Intro

## *What Is This?*

When I decided to write this book, the first thing that came to mind was what it would *not* be about. Though *In Love And College* is geared toward college students, it is not a guide to picking up women or men through tactics. It is not about playing "the game" or using manipulative means to score phone numbers, dates, or sex. Most importantly, this book is not for those who aren't interested in commitment.

Yes, commitment. It's a scary word to a young adult who's supposedly still in the process of self-discovery. It's too binding of a word for those who believe college is about seeking pleasure and experimenting with multiple partners. The word is not in the vocabulary of men or women who fear that settling down too early will ruin the so-called "best years" of their lives.

Not only do many people steer away from actively seeking a relationship, but they also shun any opportunity for commitment. And I wonder: Are they cheating themselves out of true happiness, the kind that comes without the attachment of social stereotypes?

This book has been written with the mindset that beneath many of the hard-shelled, commitment-fearing souls, there are plenty of men and women who want to love and be loved. But we aren't all the same. For example, there are some who openly express their desire for commitment and wish there was a practical means of success. Then there are the inexperienced, who want what they feel is all but unattainable.

All of the text you'll find within these pages is based on personal experience and research. I have been a relationship advice columnist for quite some time, but during and before that chapter in my life, I have interacted with hundreds of college-age couples from all parts of the United States. I made it my mission to learn about this anomaly known as commitment in college. Through my experiences, I've discovered one important thing: There is no such thing as a frivolous problem.

Something as silly as a bad Christmas gift or a conflict about public display of affection has been known to end a relationship that would have otherwise been successful. It's all because the couple was unable to communicate their feelings and ideals until it was too late – and some never even get that far.

I've tried to cover a wide range of relationship issues in this book, many of which cite examples from letter submissions and conversations I've had with other couples. Topics range from abuse and infidelity to living together and maintaining a long-term bond after the initial giddiness of a new relationship wears off.

The book is divided into six chapters, and each chapter contains segments that cover specific topics. While the segments comprise a bigger idea in regards to the stages of a relationship, I've written them so that each one can stand alone. You don't have to read the book from front to back, but it's much more fun that way. I hope you enjoy reading this practical guide to practical relationships as much as I enjoyed writing it.

My goal has always been to provide a practical, straight-

Introduction

forward guide that leaves you with the freedom to make your own educated decisions. If there is something in this book that strikes you as odd, or if you outright disagree with my opinion on a certain topic, I am interested in what you have to say. I urge you to e-mail me about it at InLoveAndCollege@gmail.com.

There is much more to love and relationships than what you will find in this book, but it will go a long way in helping you understand how and why every couple is different. There are no hard and fast rules for making your love life more successful than someone else's – just guidelines to give you a fighting chance.

# 1

# Before You Jump

The first chapter is aptly named "Before You Jump," because jumping into the dating scene without knowing what you want from a relationship is the easiest way to wind up in a vicious cycle of needless searching. How will your views about sex affect your pursuit of love? Are you looking for a soul mate? Is it worth pursuing a long-time friend, knowing the risks involved if it doesn't work out? Can you handle rejection?

They are questions we all have to face, and the answers will lead to decisions only you can make. This chapter helps you get past the common inhibitions involved in actively seeking a relationship. It begins with a bit of insight about virginity and its affect on a relationship, followed by a segment that clears the air about compatibility. The chapter ends with a note about what it means to hold important standards and compromise the rest.

Having a sense of certainty when it comes to finding and choosing a mate brings you more than just a good partner; it brings you the satisfaction that you did it without anyone else's help.

## *Are You Waiting Until Marriage?*

IF YOU are, you needn't be commended nor looked down upon. This is your personal decision to remain a virgin until marriage, and I hope it isn't for the sake of appearance, superiority, recognition, or religion. Everyone is entitled to personal morals and beliefs, but the key is to make sure it's what *you* want and not what someone else expects of you.

I say that because while there are a few people nowadays who don't see sex as important and hardly care whether they're having it or not, most people want it and consider sexual compatibility part of the foundation of a successful relationship. And for good reason, because not only is sex fun, but it also satisfies our most basic instincts. The choice to save sex for your husband or wife seems to primarily stem from religion, but some of the very few who still hold these values actually do it for personal reasons that might involve past experiences.

Like all standards, the decision to stay a virgin will limit your prospects, effectively eliminating those who would otherwise be good matches for you. Some people love sex too much to give it up for someone. Others might try but ultimately end up miserable, and there are those who just don't support your reason behind waiting until marriage. The ideal mate for you is probably a person who also wants to wait, because security and trust will be significantly easier to attain early in the relationship.

The argument against those who wait until marriage is that waiting too long can bring a lot of disappointment. A couple could be in love for years and years, but on their wedding night they could discover they can't transfer that same chemistry into the bedroom. Their "sexual auras" are not in sync; they simply aren't sexually compatible. It's not surprising to know that this is just a weak excuse heard all around the world.

Consider this: If you've made it to marriage, you've successfully become emotionally intimate with your partner. Your relationship has withstood the test of time and both of you – we can only hope – have decided you are ready for that semi-lifelong commitment of marriage. Is additional physical intimacy going to be the *one* problem you failed to overcome? The answer is no. Sex is just another thing you're trying as a couple – another thing to talk about and another thing to perfect and enjoy. It involves communication skills, emotional connection, and consideration. As husband and wife, none of those things should be difficult, and if they are, take a break from sex and see a counselor to figure out the real issues.

A relationship cannot exist without intimacy, but the college crowd incorrectly defines intimacy as completely sexual. Those who choose to remain virgins, however, might understand that intimacy is more than physical. It is full-fledged synergy. It's sharing one another's lives mentally and emotionally – and hell, we can even say spiritually.

Then again, not everyone who chooses to be a virgin until marriage really cares to use that argument. To them, it's none of your business. And some of them don't even have a valid argument besides calling premarital sex "immoral" or "degrading the sanctity of it." Others believe sex is only for procreation and condemn all who use any sort of contraceptives. But those are beliefs based on the teachings of others who were also taught those beliefs. It's not worth discussing.

The best tangible example I can provide is the story of a college freshman who was surprised at how difficult it was to keep a boyfriend due to her decision to abstain from sex until the wedding night. In high school it was a non-issue, but she discovered that college relationships seemed to have different rules. When she starts really connecting with a guy and becomes exclusive with him, she drops the bombshell that she will not have premarital sex. And the guy can't handle that.

"If he truly cared about me, it would be worth the wait," she said.

But of course, there's a problem with that statement. He's a new boyfriend who has learned the painful truth that he won't be having sex with his new girlfriend anytime soon. And she's saying it should be worth the wait, which is assuming far too much for a fairly new relationship. If you use that reasoning, you're talking about the prospect of marriage with *him* when you should be focusing on the fact that you want to be a virgin *until you get married, period*. She can't assume he doesn't care about her just because he's not able to share her ideals. If sex is important to him, which it probably is, he cannot be expected to fully invest in this relationship, knowing that he would have to marry her to get what he feels he should be entitled to before that.

For many people, the concept just doesn't make sense. You wouldn't tell your boss at a new job that your quality of work will increase after your first promotion or raise, because you can't assume he will keep you around long enough for that to happen.

I'm certainly not saying that anyone who has decided to be a virgin until marriage should sacrifice their morals to keep their partner around, but I do want you to understand that it's unfair to fully discredit someone for being unable to support your decision. You are neither good nor bad for saving sex for marriage, and the same goes for people who engage in premarital sex. It's just a belief or a decision you've made, and whether you like it or not, it will limit your dating options. You can either complain about how no one seems to respect your decision, or you can accept that you will have to work harder at finding someone right for you. Part of that effort will require you to get it out in the open – early on – that you are a virgin and will remain one until the honeymoon. Maybe it's not something to bring up on the first date (unless an opportunity presents itself), but it needs to be said before anything gets even remotely serious.

If you've stood strong in your decision, you deserve someone who will respect it and be willing to wait. And even though others couldn't accept your choices, you have shown that in at least one aspect of your life, you are quite strong-willed. But if you think that, alone, makes you better than anyone else, you are sadly mistaken.

## What Is Compatibility?

A SHARP POINT that has jabbed at me in the last half decade is the issue of compatibility. What does it mean, anyway, to be compatible with someone? Can we be compatible with a person who has different political or religious beliefs? Is it possible for people with conflicting personalities to live happily ever after?

The first time I was introduced to a philosophy of compatibility, it came in the form of a Valentine's Day fundraiser at my high school. We were invited to take a personality and interests test, the results of which would be compared with other students of the opposite sex in our grade and other grades. If you wanted to see who matched up best with your answers, all you had to do was wait until the day before Valentine's Day and pay a dollar for the results. One sheet listed the ten people who were most "compatible" with you in your grade. The other sheet consisted of your top ten matches from other grades. As a single teenager with raging hormones, I definitely paid my dollar.

I went to high school with my now long-term partner, and she was never on any of my lists. The girls who were apparently most compatible with me had no idea who I was, and vice versa. I went on a date with one of the girls, actually, based on those one-dollar results. It was boring, aside from the small talk we were able to conjure from the whole match-making process. She was a good friend at best, but romance? No way.

Obviously, I can't say that one unsuccessful date makes the whole list null and void, but the main thing I learned about compatibility was how horribly wrong I was by thinking shared interests were a top priority.

Imagine the typical sour-date scenario: Two people sit at dinner, completely incapable of engaging in conversation for more than a few multi-second bursts at a time. Sitting in on this "conversation," we could learn that she wants to be a lounge singer and he hates jazz. He fixes computers for fun and she writes poetry.

They sit in silence and poke at their food a bit. He checks his cell phone to pretend like he got a text message and escape the situation briefly. She brings up the topic of TV shows. They smile, excited for a second because they both enjoy the same program, but then they quickly find out it's for different reasons. And the conversation dwindles again.

Out of desperation, they change the subject to school. But he's a computer science senior, and she's an undecided sophomore leaning toward English.

"Oh," he says.

"Yeah," replies his date.

"I couldn't imagine doing anything that wasn't on a computer," he says with a half-hearted chuckle.

"Heh, heh."

And that conversation dies, too. The date comes to a close, and that's too bad.

What went wrong here?

If you're thinking they simply didn't have anything in common, you're only partially right. The couple might be on different paths in life and follow different hobbies and interests, but what makes that an issue of incompatibility?

He stated his interests, and she stated hers. They both acknowledged that each had contributed equally to the conversation. But it's more important to note that clearly neither of them knew a damned thing about each other's career paths or subjects of interest. Why not make a conversation out of that? It's because they just weren't interested in each other, and it's nobody's fault.

This is where I might lose a lot of you with my less-than-scientific logic. In my own warped and tragically unpoetic mind, I see human personalities interacting a lot like two automobiles speeding toward each other for a high-speed head-on collision of death. Yay!

We produce vibes (spiritual auras or auditory and/or visual displays – take your pick) that tell a person who we are without having to do much talking. It's the same way a writer deals with characterization sans dialogue and exposition. We have personalities that present themselves the same way, but what varies is how our vibes are received. If your vibe is a lot like a freight train interacting with someone who gives off the vibe of a scooter, someone dies in that collision. Did I lose you with the metaphor? Let me start over.

In that date scenario I described, they could have talked for hours to learn about their respective interests and fields, but they chose not to do that because someone – or both – was bored. This means a personality or two was not well-received. Some people can't stand to be around others who don't share the same goals and beliefs as they do. Some people don't know how to interact with different personality types. Others are simply afraid of being boring or, conversely, revealing too much on the first date. Some people hate talking, and others hate listening.

But the point I want to make is that we all have to find these things out through experience. Dating sites and other services with "compatibility" quizzes give people the ill-conceived notion that matching a few answers can find your "equal" and bring you the love of your life. It can indeed, but the best of these services will even explain that it's not for everyone. I believe it's not for most people. I believe most people cannot sustain a long-term relationship with their mental and emotional equal. Honestly, ask yourself whether you'd date the opposite-sex version of you, and think about it for at least a minute.

Above all, you must realize that compatibility is not about both of you liking The Rolling Stones better than The Beatles or sharing some obscure childhood ritual. These are things to laugh about, or to break the ice to get things moving, but they are certainly not the glue for everlasting love. Interests are important, but so many people make the mistake of waiting for that "special someone" who mirrors exactly who they are instead of the true special someone who *appreciates* who they are. Personally, I think I'm quite the overbearing bastard, and another one of me would probably destroy the universe if it got too close.

I do want to point out that there are some interests which are more important than others. But, I would be inclined to call the important stuff more of an aspect of your lifestyle. You have to accept your partner's lifestyle while still retaining the ability to implement your own – otherwise, your life will collide with his, and you aren't compatible enough to survive as a couple. For example, consider the ideals that cause debates among opinion-happy college students across the world: Of course, I'm talking about religion and politics.

Yes, a liberal and a conservative can live in perfect harmony, and a moderate and a libertarian can grow old together. But this is only possible if both parties are not infantile enough to poorly stereotype people with certain political stances. For those of you who are able to see the world like an adult, I can only tell you to tread carefully when dating people with strong religious or political beliefs. Don't let it rule the conversation. Moreover, don't let it rule your life. If you've rendered yourself incapable of falling in love with someone who worships a different god than yours, you're limiting yourself and cutting your chances of being in an optimal relationship. If that's OK with you, it's certainly OK with me.

But before you hand a company your money for love, understand that you can find a suitable mate without having to answer objective questions on a dating Web site. Next time you're on a date, just stop asking what, and try asking who, when, where, and why.

## *The F Word*

MANY ACTIVE daters seem to be set on finding their one true love, and – at the risk of sounding sexist – I've found this to be especially true with women. It seems to be all about locating the one person who will love her for who she is on the inside. She wants to find a warm body and call it her soul mate – because god only made one person for each of us. Fate will bring the two life partners together. Forever and ever. Until divorce do they part.

Seems like a lot of pressure to me, to expect to find that special someone in a reasonable amount of time. But I've been told it's all fate's doing when we bump into that girl at a pretentious coffee shop and start talking about indie music. Or it's fate when you intend to go home with the hottest girl at the bar, but you slip the drug in another girl's drink, and the two of you totally hit it off. An angel rerouted that roofie!

Some people don't get married until they're over 30 years old. Some don't even date during that time. But then two 30-somethings find each other at Wal-Mart and they're married in a month. It was fate. Fate seems to play a huge role in love once you've actually found a mate, and I'll bet that fate works a lot faster as you get older. I'm skeptical of this whole thing.

I find it amazing that fate can play a role in breakups, too. It was fate that two people got married, but the divorce is fate, too. It means fate had other plans, or they were wrong about fate. Apparently, there's nothing more infallible than fate because no matter how horribly wrong a relationship can go, we can just say that fate will bring us our real soul mate one day.

Just imagine all the crazy justifications made using fate: "It wasn't my fault, right? Something inside me told me to sleep with her sister. I think it was…fate. Never mind that her sister is already married to her soul mate, also courtesy of fate." Fate says she shouldn't tell her husband about the affair, but it looks like fate told someone else to tell him. Now they will get a divorce. Who was responsible for all this heartache?

"No, it's not heartache, silly. It's fate."

I could make fun of fate for the rest of this book, and some might say I'm pessimistic about religion in general. And they might be right. I don't believe in fate because I am banking on the fact that I only have one life, and I need to make sure I'm getting everything out of it that I deserve. To live life to its fullest, I have no choice but to believe in choice.

I drink black coffee as a write this. I could've added sugar or milk. I could've made tea instead. Or I could've thrown the coffee pot at one of my cats because cats piss me off. I could still change my mind and do any of those things. My choices would affect my current mood, and my current mood would affect what I write. You could be reading something different on this page had I attacked my cat or decided to write without caffeine. Does fate decide what I write?

I was told that fate has a plan. Anything and everything I do is because I'm destined to be somewhere and do something at some point in time – which ultimately leads me to do something else that fate planned for me. I just don't buy it.

Love can't be based on fate. Our mistakes in relationships can't be the result of fate trying to teach us a lesson – because what is the point of learning anything if fate has already decided where we will go and where we will end? And no, I'm not trying to sound deep; I'm trying to tell you that fate isn't why you are where you are. If you want to be in a relationship, choose to be in a relationship.

People often make the mistake of meeting a good person and waiting for him to give off a clear-cut vibe that he's interested.

Right, because it always works like that.

How many potential relationships will you pass over until you realize you are in control? How long until you realize that both sexes are guilty of waiting for a man or woman to make the first move?

There is more than one person out there for everyone. I've said this many times throughout my years of giving advice, but everyone seems to think that the person you grow old and die with is the one who was meant for you.

Oh, and it gets worse.

In another advice column, I read about a woman in an emotionally abusive relationship who refused to leave on the grounds that god had intentionally brought the abusive man in her life so she can help "reform" him. And of course, there have been women who sought advice from me about whether or not their boyfriends were "the one."

"I love him, but I want to make sure he is *it*."

I ask, "Does he make you happy?"

"Yes."

"Good sex?"

"Yeah," (insert shy laughter.)

"He's the one."

And they have the nerve to call me a hack.

Fate is not responsible for the high divorce rate in the United States. Poor decision-making is. Select your mate like you select your brand of coffee. And if that coffee is everything you want and need, you stick with it. You can drink it your entire life and be perfectly content with it – even though there's a brand out there that's just as good, but you never thought of trying it.

But who gives a damn? I love my coffee.

## *How Can You Tell?*

"DEAR STEPHEN, how do you know if a [guy/girl] likes you?"

I can't answer this question anymore. I believe that if every good advice columnist had it his or her way, this question would be stricken from the pages forever. In fact, the phrase "how do you know" might even be banned from existence if left up to me. The truth is, we shouldn't even ask another person how to "know" whether someone is interested in us. There are no real accurate signs, but a few relationship advicists have tried to make some up. Most advice given by radio personalities, talk show hosts, and columnists usually falls on filtered ears, so it has become easier to tell others what they want to hear. Thus, such advice has evolved into generic, frivolous garbage that slips right by that filter and makes the reader or the caller smile and say, "Thanks, that's what I thought."

From a generic advice-giver, some of the so-called signs that a person is interested include dilated pupils, excessive eye contact and touching, nervousness, smiling, teasing from friends, overly nice gestures, and I swear someone even told a reader to ask her spirit guide for the right signs. I'm not going to say these are wrong, but they are hardly helpful. It's like asking someone how to tell if a guy is about to rob the quickie mart. I can imagine the answer would go something like this:

> *Dear Cashier Without A Clue,*
>
> *There are many signs to tell whether that mysterious cloaked man is going to rob you. What you need to do, my dear, is open your eyes as wide as your heart before you have to open that cash register! Teehee, I just scared six of my cats by laughing out loud at my fabulous tongue-in-cheek antics. I'm certainly glad I don't have a husband, because he would think I was just cur-razy!*
>
> *Now, if you want to really know what Mr. Wrong is about to do in your store, look for these signs:*

*1) Is he wearing a black ski-mask? This is a red flag. Get out of there and back home to your kitty cats and chocolate cake!*

*2) Does he show no emotion whatsoever? This might just be because he's a man, but it's suspicious nonetheless!*

*3) Do you see the outline of a gun anywhere on his clothing? He could use a gun to threaten you or even shoot you!*

*I hope this helps. Now go out there and be a hero!*

I would hope most cashiers know the obvious signs of a suspicious-looking customer. But what about the average Joe in jeans and sneakers who pulls out a gun from his windbreaker? Nothing can prepare you for that. It's a shame the clueless cashier didn't ask *what to do* if she's being robbed.

I'll admit that part of my logic for refusing to answer the "how can you tell?" question is fear. It scares me, not only because all people are different and body language and actions vary among each of us, but also because people aren't always truthful. By that, I mean a person might show all the "right signs," but he's really just screwing with your head for the sake of enjoyment. Both men and women are guilty of it.

Give me a few signs and I'll try to interpret them for you, but you have to use your own intuition. If you tell me something basic like, "He really seems to show interest in my life," I'll tell you it's nice. But I won't tell you he likes you.

You can tell me he made dinner and delivered it to you when you were sick, and I still can't tell you he likes you. I can speculate he wants something from you, but it's not necessarily a relationship

17

or even a date. Hell, he might even want to gain your trust so he can kill you in your sleep. That's kind of where your intuition comes in. Decide what you think he wants from you, and leave the love doctors out of it.

When a friend of mine once again entered single life after ending a three-year relationship, she brought up the issue of how impersonal the world had become since she last dated other men. Her new dates were mostly communicating with her via text message and e-mail instead of a simple phone call. What happened to common courtesy, she wondered. But more important was her follow-up question: Does it mean they aren't interested?

Well, it could mean that – but again, it's not safe to make the assumption. I told her that if he texts her more often than he calls her, he might not be a keeper. What I didn't say, however, was whether or not he was interested in her. My friend, through her frustration with texting, had made it clear she valued a man who would take the time to call her. Either this guy really wasn't interested, or he was just a fan of texting over dialing. Neither of these possibilities was in my friend's best interest. And I know what you're thinking: Why not at least give the guy a chance? Answer: Because everyone is entitled to at least a few superficial standards (See page 31).

No one can, or should, tell you how to figure out who's interested in you. We're all different. If a man left you a love poem on your front door in the middle of the night, one person might tell you he's a sweet romantic who's madly in love with you, while someone else could tell you he might be mentally disturbed and have a distorted view of his connection with you. Are you going to choose between these two opinions?

If you asked me about the guy in question, I wouldn't tell you his intentions, but rather ask you if his gesture was in your comfort zone. If it freaked you out, that's probably not a good start. Only you can decide that.

So, communicate! Not with me, and not with some other advice columnist who will give you a more satisfying answer – communicate with *him*. Do you think he's interested in you?

"That's the problem; I don't know," you say.

Fair enough, but are you interested in him?

If so, *do* something about it for god's sake.

## *Doing Something About It*

WHILE KNOWING how to smooth-talk someone into giving you a phone number is a nice skill to have, what's more important is the courage to approach that person and present yourself for who you are.

If you have no idea what to do, how to act, what to say, what to wear, and so on, feel free to read the thousands of books and articles about impressing the opposite sex. You can learn about how it's done in other cultures; you can read all about the mating calls of other animals. You can learn how to manipulate a person to give you whatever you want, if such things interest you. Dating and pick-up guides will teach you how to get out of your comfort zone and interact with people you never dreamed of meeting. In a few weeks, your head could be packed with everything you would ever need to know about talking to men and women. Do you have the courage to use that information?

Much of this book could be spent talking about the different methods of pursuing someone you are interested in dating, but the key is willingness. For example, when I get a question from a woman who wonders whether guys like it if girls make the first move, I feel bad for her. It usually means she's in a situation where there's obviously a mutual attraction, but neither of them has made the effort to do anything about it. Or maybe she's doing some sort of mating dance, and she's confused as to why he has not responded.

Who is more obligated to make the first move? In a perfect world, two people would be attracted to each other at the same time and would make a move at the same time, thus reaffirming that both people are equally interested. Of course, that's not what going on a date is usually about.

To ask someone on a date is to say, "An aspect of your looks or personality has drawn me to you. Can we go to a traditionally intimate setting so we can see whether or not we find each other interesting?"

In fact, try that line on someone and see if it works. That's about all I can offer you in the realm of approaching someone for a date. I recommend you state your interest, be yourself while selling yourself, and thank the person for his or her time.

Or is that for job applications? I forget.

No matter how you get someone to go on a date with you, the most important thing to know is that it's up to you to do it. Make your decision now, because waiting for someone to come along and make the move to test the waters with you severely limits your potential for maximizing the quality of your long-term relationships. In other words, having guts gives you more choices.

Some people have spent so much time trying to master the art of scoring dates and phone numbers that they've completely forgotten how to be themselves on a date – which is fine if you're simply looking to get laid, but if you've read past the first page, I assume we can rule that out.

Being the best version of yourself on the first date is crucial. Everyone has quirks, and ideally we would be upfront about our excess baggage in the beginning – but life doesn't work like that. So, as a compromise, just take a vow of passive honesty. Show your polite side, but don't kid yourself into thinking you can keep it up for more than a few dates.

The taboo subjects on a date are obvious, but for the select few who are scratching their heads in confusion, I will clarify that being yourself does not mean you should make all your intentions clear. If you want to get married and have kids one day, that's wonderful. However, it's a taboo first-date topic among many others, like past relationships and deeply personal questions.

There might be dozens of first-date rules and tips out there, but it's still not rocket science, and those who are in pursuit of a mate should realize that a connection is imminent regardless of the occasional slip-up in conversation. You can perfect your conversational techniques all you want, but you will still seem uninteresting to some people. Get over it and try someone else, because your goal is not to trick someone into being your Mr. Right.

On the other side of the spectrum, let's try to be a little more forgiving of our dates. We are all guilty of judging people too harshly, and if such an attitude is applied to dating, we can prematurely end a courtship with someone who may or may not have had potential.

I do advocate being a picky dater, but not too picky. The first impression, though important, is not always someone's proudest moment. You might be experienced in the dating department, but your date, bless his heart, barely has any experience eating with another human. Think about your own state of mind when you try to make a good first impression. Most of us would appreciate a little slack from time to time, and I'm sure you would, too.

College students sometimes get the mindset that they are too young to tolerate anything less than perfect. Some have even told me they break contact with a person after he makes one mistake. Yikes.

Remember that your date isn't psychic; he doesn't know what you want, and he sure as hell doesn't know what kind of mental image you have of how the date or even the next few dates will play out. Similarly, you aren't psychic either. You can't predict the future, so why assume that one little slip-up is the ultimate sign that the relationship is doomed? If you're counting someone's mistakes, at least use a three-strike system. If he gets too personal with you too soon, strike one. If he doesn't open the door for you at all during the date, strike two. If he waits too long to call you back, strike three. If he apologizes for all those mistakes, strike two-ish.

If he gets angry and argues with you, strike nineteen.

## *An Age-Old Predicament*

TWO PEOPLE are interested in you and you're faced with a dilemma about who to choose. So what do you do? You ask someone else who she'd pick if in your situation. And then you ignore the advice, because what does she know? She probably just wants [name] all to herself! That bitch.

Just don't ask anyone, and save yourself the hassle.

The scenario is almost always the same: Two romantic interests oppose each other in personality, and each one lacks a quality that the other one has. You wish they could just merge into one super boyfriend. But since that's not possible, you hope to date one and remain friends with the other, just in case it doesn't work out with your first choice.

I know this situation sounds pretty high school-ish for a book about college relationships, but it has to be addressed. The first time I was faced with this question was when a 13-year-old girl asked me about it in an e-mail. I had to be very careful about my answer. She was interested in two boys who were also interested in her. One was 13 years old, and the other, disturbingly, was 17. She reasoned that she loved the maturity of the 17-year-old but valued the fact that the 13-year-old had more in common with her.

My choice for her was almost entirely based on age, obviously. It was easy because she's still a child. You just don't tell an eighth-grader to date a 17-year-old boy. I told the young girl that based on her description, the 13-year-old seemed more level-headed and "nicer." I almost wanted to tell her I heard bad things about the 17-year-old, because she probably would have believed me.

After sending the message, I distinctly remember saying aloud, "I'm so glad that wasn't from a college student."

Three days later, I got one from a college student. We'll call her "Sally."

Sally's predicament was about choosing between her best friend and a man she just met. And she ended her letter with, "Which one should I choose?"

I dreaded getting this question from anyone older than 17 because I thought that would mean I was wrong about the maturity level of college relationships. But then I realized that no matter how mature you are, you're never too old to be afraid to make the wrong choice. And that's what she feared – hurting someone and regretting her choice.

The cookie-cutter answer for Sally's question would be to go with whom she feels has the most potential to be a long-term mate. While one guy is new, the friend has stood the test of time with her – but watch out, as the friend might be better suited to stick to his role. A breakup could result in the loss of a friend, while a relationship with the new guy has less risk.

But that's not what I told her.

The previous advice doesn't help her, since we have to assume she's smart enough to realize the pros and cons of dating either of them. And if she didn't know she's at risk for losing her friend by dating him, she probably could have Googled it.

Other generic advice might say she should go with her heart and be prepared to hurt someone, but I don't agree with that, either. She should not pick either of them. Seems like unhelpful advice, and I realize that. Keep reading.

In dating, I always encourage you to look out for your own best interests, and only associate yourself with those who can enrich your life. But, we often have to consider the feelings of others for our own sake.

If Sally chooses the new guy – we'll call him "Peter" – her friendship with the long-time pal – whom we'll call "John" – will be strained. If both men are actively vying for her affection, there is a winner and a loser. No one likes to lose, and John will probably resent Sally and view it as her failure to notice how much effort and emotional investment he has given to maintain a bond with her for X amount of months or years. In his mind, Sally has made a superficial decision to pursue something new and exciting without appreciating the value of friendship and devotion. It's likely that throughout the short-lived relationship with Peter, John will distance himself from her – or worse, try to sabotage the relationship. Sally won't have time to regret her decision to choose Peter, because John will no longer present himself as a viable option.

But what if Sally chooses John, her good friend who knows her inside and out and has been with her through even the most painful and awkward moments? It's obvious the bond is there, and if Sally is sexually attracted to him, we're all set for one of those "Super-Couples" I've been hearing all about.

The consensus among most experienced daters is that dating a close friend is too risky, because if you break up, the friendship will probably be over. Breakups are rarely mutual, so somebody is going to be dissatisfied with the way things ended, which will ultimately take the friendship down a few notches.

I've said this before and received countless responses from people who claimed to have dated their best friends, broke up with them, and continued to be the best of pals. This proves nothing, because none of them would be able to tell me how their exes *really* feel about the breakup. What seems like the same friendship on the surface can be something quite nasty underneath. If Sally and John break up, John might still have lingering feelings for Sally, but Sally has moved on. In that situation, Sally has taken a longer route to scenario one, where she had picked the new guy, Peter, and John inevitably faded away. If Sally has lingering feelings for John, but John realized he was better off as the best friend, Sally cries hypocrisy. How dare *he* break up with *her*, when he wanted this all along?

But even if, through all of that, Sally and John managed to remain close, sans bitterness, they still have to deal with the baggage of having an ex for a best friend. But that's an entirely different topic.

Sally needs more time to make this decision, taking that time alone – the key idea here being, "I want to stay single for a while." If she's strongly attracted to both prospects and is looking for a meaningful relationship, she should not have a problem slowing down her selection process. One will shine brighter than the other, eventually.

During this time, however, Sally should understand that this is not an opportunity to objectify the situation or milk the attention from these men. Instead, she needs to take time to herself and realize that neither of the men should be happy about competing for her affection. In fact, if Peter or John had come to me for advice about whether it's worth it, I'd have to tell them it isn't. I worry that people who have to decide between two prospects will end up wondering what would've happened if they had made a different decision, and that hinders their full investment in the current relationship. It's just not a good situation sometimes.

Even so, Sally has the right to see who is most patient, just for her own well-being. It's up to her whether she will be fully committed to her decision or not.

In the end, I'd predict that Peter is not as patient as John. And now Sally's choice is easier, provided other men haven't entered her life during the inevitable phasing out of Peter. If John was a worthy candidate for her affection in the first place, he'll still be there – same old best friend John. If Sally was considerate during her selection process, this should be seen as a test of staying power and not a sneaky plot to get rid of Peter and avoid confrontation. Peter could just as well be the guy who sticks around, while best friend John gets fed up and moves on. Or they both might move on. You can't blame either of them for giving up, obviously. The point of this waiting game is not to inflate Sally's ego, but to break the tension of male rivalry. Eventually, John and Peter would find out about each other if they had not already. From my experience, that kind of pressure does not a good relationship make.

After speaking with several women on this subject, it seems that the ideal dating prospect is someone who's a friend, but hasn't been a friend for very long – the median of best friend and new acquaintance. The risk and the tension are both low, and these are the most favorable conditions. But again, it depends on the type of person you are. There are plenty of people who prefer either one or the other extreme: new and exciting, or safe and familiar.

Sally ended up picking John, by the way, and Peter quickly and gracefully moved on. As for what will come of Sally and John's newfound romantic bond, that is yet to be determined. She knows the risks involved in dating a good friend, as does everyone else. But all the Sallies of the world should never let such a risk prevent you from taking the leap into romance with their own Johns. You might miss something amazing, and that is not worth risking.

## *Rejection Is A Bitch*

THE TITLE says it all, and the best way to start off this segment is with a nice, heartfelt e-mail a reader sent to me:

*Dear Stephen,*

*I've been rejected for the last time. I'm done with approaching women. I'm sick of putting myself out there and getting torn down, every fucking time. I am tired of trying to adhere to society's standards to the letter, just so I can get a date. I don't want to go through another first date which is never followed by a second.*

*It seems that no matter how hard I try, I just can't impress a girl long enough to get more than one date, if that. Usually, they just politely say no and move on. But the ones who give me a chance are always turned off by me when I ac-*

27

*tually try to be myself on a date.*

*What is wrong with society these days? Whatever happened to appreciating a person's imperfections?*

*- Rejected*

A few queries come to mind: (1) What kinds of women has this guy been chasing? (2) How will he ever find love with that attitude? And (3) What is it about him that turns women off?

My reply:

Dear Rejected,

We've all been there in one way or another. We've been denied admission, loans, raises, promotions, awards, etc. It's worse, however, when you get rejected as a person rather than a number. If we look at all of our rejections as a single entity, it makes us seem like massive failures. So look at your rejections individually instead. They aren't failures or reasons to give up. They are quite the opposite.

Rejections might mean you need to try again. They might mean that the woman you were after is not a match. Whether she says no outright or just doesn't want a second date, you know she's not your type. Your type is someone who will not only give you a chance, but also be glad she did. Is it her loss for rejecting you? Not at all. You weren't her type, either.

It's too easy to say that those who reject us aren't good enough for us, but the reality is we weren't "good enough" for them – or at least not right for them. We all need the ability to turn someone down, or else we will waste too much time with the ones we know we don't want.

Of course, not everyone is nice about the rejection. Some people can be outright offended that you even bothered to ask them on a date. Others will expound on the simple "no" by telling you that no one would date you if you were the last man on Earth. Perhaps some will even give constructive feedback as a qualifier for rejecting you.

Having said that, have you ever wondered why you're being rejected – like an actual *why*, sans the anti-society hogwash? There's always a reason, and sometimes it's a very good reason that isn't necessarily superficial.

If you honestly believe there's no hope for you at this point, I recommend taking a break from the game and having some practice runs. Get a few doses of honesty from a trusted friend. There could be something about your approach that turns most women off, and perhaps your date etiquette isn't up to snuff.

People might tell you not to worry and that you will find someone eventually, but it will be a heck of a lot harder if you aren't correctly sending the intended signals. Or if you don't shower.

Remember, however, that you still must make your own decisions. You may benefit from a lesson in dating, but that doesn't mean you need to follow any sort of set formula. If something doesn't feel right, don't do it.

And stop blaming the world as if it's going to change.

The idea was to nicely tell him he should consider the possibility that he's an obnoxious idiot. On top of that, he should be intuitive enough to weed out the obvious superficial rejections and consider the ones that offer hidden insight. The types of women he's been after could greatly affect the amount of rejections he's getting. Just because you're interested in a certain personality type does not mean it's the right one for you. Some people have to learn this the hard way.

"Rejected" should also realize that after being alone for so long, he probably emanates the "I need to date someone now!" vibe, which is always a huge turn-off. Needy translates into codependence. Every advice columnist in the world will tell you to show a potential mate that you are a happy, independent person with or without a partner. I agree.

Setting yourself up for rejection is easy, and so is believing your rejections come from the fact that no one understands you. That is how people try to cope with being alone, as if being alone means they cannot be happy. You might be comfortable with yourself and how you look and feel, but that's only half of the requirements. You have to be comfortable with the rest of the world, even the part that rejects you.

Instead of viewing your rejections as a sentence to loneliness, consider a significant other as the icing on the cake that is your already-successful, happy, independent life.

## *Fitting Your Standards*

HAVE YOU ever been called superficial? Maybe someone thought you were being unfair when you refused to date his friend because he smokes. Or someone might have said you're too judgmental because you didn't give a guy a chance due to his height or weight or religion or hairstyle. But you argue that you just have certain standards you aren't willing to sacrifice – which is OK, as long as you don't have too many.

There are superficial standards, and there are lifestyle standards. Superficial standards are those aesthetic preferences you have, as well as a few preferable personality quirks. It's the stuff that kind of matters but can be overlooked for the right person. The lifestyle standards are bigger; they're the qualities that affect the way a person lives – a lifestyle that will *always* carry over to a relationship.

 Sometimes it's hard to figure out under which category to place your standards. Height, for example, is often misconstrued as a non-negotiable standard. Some people say they can't have a mate who's taller than they are. It's intimidating and awkward, and the fit just wouldn't seem right. And having someone who's too short compared to you will seem silly in public. But I think it's a superficial standard by any definition; height is relative. You are certainly allowed to disagree with me, however. They're your standards, not mine.

Dating based on a person's job is ultimately a superficial standard if you discriminate against people who have less-than-glamorous jobs. I suppose this becomes a more important standard as we get older, but in college, your partner's job is probably going to kind of suck, and so is yours.

And then there's income – we want someone with ambition, which might make us believe that income is a lifestyle standard. However, putting too much emphasis on finding a person who fits a certain income profile will lead to trouble down the road. Your partner probably won't always make the same amount of money. Keep character in check, but the bank account is not your business for now.

Of course, there are the obvious superficial standards, like facial features, various tastes, voice, laughing style, finger length, hair color, shoe size, body hair, and so on and so on.

But I don't have to preach to you about compromising these standards in the name of love, or at least in the name of a fling if it ends up as such. Hopefully, you were taught at an early age that it's what's on the inside that counts. By junior high that sentiment had been forgotten, and then by college you figured out some kind of compromise between the two ideals. You now understand that romantic love cannot exist without sexual attraction.

So perhaps we are allowed a bit of superficiality in dating without going overboard. Don't date the guy who is proud of his beard if beards bother you; avoid him if he laughs obnoxiously loud no matter where he is. But before you make that decision, see what kind of lifestyle standards these prospects fit:

1. Smoking and drugs – If you don't approve of these, it will be a difficult standard to overlook. Addiction is a lifestyle that affects more than the person who is addicted. Smokers will need smoke breaks during extended activities. Drug users can and probably will put you second to their habit.

2. Alcohol – While drinkers probably don't have an addiction, it's not something they are going to give up just to fit your standards. If you don't want alcohol to be a part of your life in any way, you won't be able to date – or change – a drinker.

3. Trust – This is a standard everyone should have. A person who lies to other people in front of you will probably end up telling *you* a few lies along the way, too. You're a new partner; what makes you immune?

4. Patience – Pushy is bad. Being a pushover is worse. Someone who has a grasp on maintaining that middle ground would be an ideal mate. Seeking a person who knows what he wants and can get it respectfully is a good standard to have.

There are plenty more lifestyle standards I could discuss – like views on diet and exercise, strong religious ideals, vast cultural differences, sexual experience – but the general idea to get from this is that most of these "lifestyle standards" should be non-negotiable. The ones listed above are obvious and general, but they can get specific and they can seem ridiculous to others. However, it's your relationship, and the success of it will depend on how capable you are of dealing with those qualities in your partner that don't exactly meet your original standards.

I know plenty of people who have made the mistake of compromising a lifestyle standard in favor of a prospect who fulfilled almost all of their superficial standards. Maybe he had a bit of a drug problem – but he was just the right height, somehow holding down a great job, and absolutely gorgeous. How long do you think it will be before the looks and the money become a little less important?

If you feel comfortable with taking the risk, then by all means go for it. However, time and observation have proven that people who are unhappy with the way their partner lives his life are ultimately unhappy in the relationship – duh.

You just have to get your priorities straight: A non-drinker who is untrustworthy, an honest guy who is too aggressive, or maybe a dieting, exercising alcoholic – do these people seem desirable?

I do want to add that your lifestyle standards can change. While you might not be a health nut now, you could be more inclined to tolerate or even participate if your partner one day decides to diet and exercise more. Some couples start off with similar beliefs, but one partner might begin to have doubts about religion and stop going to church, or the less-religious could find their faith. It's much easier to accept and tolerate these lifestyle changes once you are in love. It's easier to accept how a person grows with you. It's also a requirement.

But never should you go into a relationship hoping that you'll be able to overlook the life choices someone has already made – or worse, hoping that you'll be able to change those choices. When you enter that realm of couple-hood, you are agreeing that you've met each other's standards to an acceptable level. You are saying you're OK with who your partner is.

You are accepting that there is no such thing as a fixer-upper relationship.

# 2

# Start Your Engines

Welcome to the easy part of the relationship: the beginning. It's the euphoria of new infatuation, the lovey-dovey stuff, the baby talk, and the incessant need to show the world how in love you are. The beginning of a relationship is truly a wonderful experience, even if it disgusts everyone else.

But to enjoy the happy stuff beyond the first few months, you have to lay a good foundation for the future. You must begin working at compromise and communication from the start, or else the sweet beginning will eventually come to a bitter end.

The person you were drawn to might not be as experienced as you are. Perhaps *you* aren't as experienced as your partner initially thought. Your new significant other might have an undesirable perception of compromise. Are you prepared to handle any of these things? Now is the time to address the questions that will ultimately determine how the rest of this relationship plays out after the initial excitement has faded.

And aside from learning to stay in tune with each other's feelings, you could stand to learn a little etiquette along the way, including a lesson in humility and a sense of when it's OK to calm down and take things in stride.

This chapter covers the most common issues that arise in the first few months of a relationship, starting with New Relationship Syndrome, a condition that makes idiots of us all. The chapter ends with a very important segment that gives a little insight on the make-or-break aspect of all relationships: compromise. Don't be a sitting duck during these glorious moments of new love. Read this chapter.

## *We're Just Jealous Of Your Love*

YOU'VE FINALLY done it. You found someone who seems to be the end-all be-all of your seemingly perpetual endeavor to find love. This new relationship is a huge attainment in your life, and you are so happy that envy itself must envy you. And to top it off, you just lost your virginity and it was the very most specialest thing that ever, ever happened. Your friends are all very happy for you, and they want to meet this new flame and have a group hangout sometime this – hey, wait, where did you go?

Millions of Americans suffer from New Relationship Syndrome (NRS) every year. It's caused by the onset of having a new significant other, and symptoms include neglecting life, friends, and most other obligations in favor of day-long sex marathons and excessive alone time with the new partner. Nothing else seems to matter to a victim of NRS.

Yes, it's a wonderful feeling to find the man or woman of your dreams. It makes you think there's nothing else to worry about ever again. It makes friends obsolete. After all, you can't make out with your friends or spend half the day arguing over who loves whom the mostest. No one else has ever felt the way you and your new sweetie feel about each other. You have a unique love that's weird but romantic, and that makes you better and stronger than any other couple.

For the sake of being happy and healthy, it's a beautiful state of mind. Just keep it to yourself, or your partner will be the only person you have in life – until, of course, you don't have him anymore, either. While I don't agree with the notion that friends are always "forever" and romances come and go, it's still a good idea to make sure you aren't needlessly cutting ties with people just because you don't need them at the moment. If you're going to lose friends, this shouldn't be how it happens.

When it comes to NRS issues, it's never the couple who seeks advice, but rather the friend who just got shut out of the couple's world. For example, when "Jack" and "Susan" started dating, Susan's best friend "Cindy" was still single and relied heavily on friends when she was in need of interaction on the weekends. Unfortunately, Susan disappeared for months. Before Jack ever came into the picture, Cindy confided in Susan and shared all of her secrets that would otherwise be in lockdown. Both women had stayed single all the way until their second year in college, and Susan was the first to meet someone. From Cindy's point of view, Jack had stolen Susan from her. Cindy no longer had her best friend, because her best friend had found someone better. Even after Susan and Jack broke up, Cindy said they could never reconcile. Given that, her question was about future prevention, not treatment.

Cindy, among the millions of people who have friends with NRS, thought this fictitious disease was Jack's fault. She thought, perhaps, that Jack was controlling or possessive and had somehow brainwashed Susan into dumping all her friends.

Not so. Susan lost control of her good judgment and time-management skills, but it wasn't because Jack made her do it. It was the buzz of being in a brand new relationship – combined with Cindy's tinge of jealousy – that ultimately ended the friendship. When Jack and Susan broke up, the relationship buzz instantly wore off, and Cindy was probably the first person Susan called to seek consolation. Unfortunately, Cindy wasn't able to forgive Susan for being so inconsiderate.

New Relationship Syndrome has different levels of intensity, and Susan's NRS was probably only moderate. If Cindy would have been more patient, they could've stayed friends. But both women were inexperienced in romance and had no idea what to expect. Susan didn't realize she would get so wrapped up in having a new boyfriend, and Cindy didn't realize why it was all happening. Also, Cindy has to admit she was jealous – all that baby talk, kissing, constant text messaging, and even those wall posts on Facebook.com; it's nauseating.

To keep a friendship from going sour like Cindy and Susan's did, there has to be patience and consideration on all sides of the relationship. Like hangovers and broken hearts, the best cure for NRS is time. During that time, friends and new couples should try their best to consider the mindsets of one another.

New couples, this is a happy time in your life, but you still have other people who care about you. It feels like heaven right now, but in a few months you will get comfortable. A kid who gets a new toy for Christmas will eventually come out of his room to see what the rest of the family is up to, just like you and your new partner will probably want to start integrating yourselves into society again.

In terrible cases of NRS, the couple emerges from the bedroom to find that they've ruined good friendships by saying regrettable things. And it's not that they don't remember saying them; they just didn't care at the time. It seemed tactful to tell your best friend that she's always been a jealous lunatic and never wants anyone else to be happy. It was the truth, right? Or maybe not so much, now that you think about it.

A lot of people realize they tend to act this way in new relationships, but mere awareness shouldn't be treated as an excuse. You should not expect your friends to ignore your unkind words or your blatant disregard for their feelings during this time. If you believe your friends are either jealous or just malicious and want to hurt your new relationship, try waiting two or three months before addressing it – or really, just ignore them for three months. That way, when you figure out how wrong you were, the friendship can remain intact.

As new couples, you should also note that NRS doesn't always affect both of you the same way. You might be infatuated with him and oblivious of everything else, but he could be staying in contact with his friends and giving himself the opportunity for quality time with other people in his life; perhaps he is taking you out with his friends regularly. In such a case, it might appear to others as though you were forced to be part of his group of friends. Of course, this is not the case. You are still too "buzzed" to care where you're being taken, and he is probably wondering why you haven't mentioned your friends, or if you even have any.

If you are a friend of an NRS victim, you have to be even more considerate. You're the one who still has control of your emotions. The only way to deal with a friend with NRS is to leave the situation alone. If she doesn't contact you, don't contact her unless you have to. Otherwise, you'll look like the pushy, jealous friend who has to meddle with everything. It will seem like you are intentionally calling your friend when you *knew* she was with her boyfriend. You're just trying to screw things up because you're lonely. Maybe you're trying to steal him! Oh my god! Get out of my life forever, you back-stabbing jezebel!

And so on. The point is, you have to avoid a potentially messy situation or you will end up looking like the villain. Once the NRS wears off, you might find that you can't forgive the horrible things your friend said when you were just trying to remain a part of her life. Though some people are more forgiving than others, *you* might end up saying something regrettable in the heat of the moment, and the friendship could be damaged on both sides.

And if you absolutely despise your friend's new mate, don't even think about mentioning it to a soul, especially your friend, unless it's evident your friend is being abused in some way or if you can present hard evidence of infidelity. You certainly can't go to her and say you think her boyfriend is cheating on her without having something that forces her to face the truth – because that would mean you're just jealous of their love. To a friend with NRS, your word is hardly valuable. In circumstances where you think your friend deserves better, you can tell her, but ultimately, she'll have to figure it out alone.

I know it doesn't seem honorable to allow a friend to get hurt when you think you can stop it, but sometimes you have to know when to keep your mouth shut and let people learn from their mistakes. It's the only clinically tested and successful treatment for New Relationship Syndrome.

## No Experience Necessary

SOME OF us are leaders, and the rest are followers. Jobs, life, relationships – it's all the same. There are those who love the idea of dating an inexperienced virgin so they can be the teacher and mold their mate into the ultimate lover, but others demand a good resume from their partner, complete with job experience and related skills. Ideally, we don't want to deviate from these standards, but sometimes it just doesn't happen that way.

The first date is not the time to discuss past relationships, but the first date is usually when the initial connection happens. And even on the second and third dates, when you realize there's a viable chance for higher romance, it's not always clear how much experience your date has with past relationships. Sure, you can tell whether he's new to dating by how he acts – or maybe he's doing a decent job because he read a lot of articles online and practiced on his sister before going out on the date. Just sayin'.

And still, plenty of men know how to treat a lady, until they get to the bedroom. Plenty of women are great in bed, but have no social skills. And, you know, vice versa.

If you've connected with a person and started a relationship, what happens when you find out that this is your new partner's very first relationship? When it comes to inexperience, the most common issues can be summed up with this great letter:

*Dear Stephen,*

*I really thought I found the one. I mean, he's an incredible guy, the freaking epitome of gorgeous, and he says all the right things. He's smooth, like yuppie-salesman smooth. Only problem is, he sucks in bed. Like, really, really bad. Getting intimate with him is kind of like approaching that sad, neglected old dog at the pound. He's so scared and confused that it's almost kind of cute, but pathetic. We didn't have sex until a month into the relationship, and that's when I discovered I was not only his first sexual partner, but his first girlfriend, and even his first "real" date.*

*What have I gotten into? I know I should be patient with him, but I don't really have time to be a mentor. I'm not exactly Miss Experience either. I'm just experienced enough to know he's terrible at all things sexual. I don't know if I feel comfortable being a teacher in the first place, and I don't want to make him feel awkward. So*

*will he improve over time? Is it all worth deal-
ing with?*

*Sincerely,
Disappointed*

To this day, I still wonder how well "Disappointed" performed during her first time. Was she just as bad at it? I can imagine so, but I also wonder if her partner was patient enough to understand. Or maybe it doesn't really matter how well she did, depending on the guy's idea of good sex.

My reply to her was brief:

Dear Disappointed,

I think you're forgetting that everyone has a "first time," and it's never as beautiful or as sexy as teen romance movies make it out to be. If there's a true connection, why on earth would you break up with him because of his lack of experience? That nervous dog at the pound isn't going to warm up to you more quickly just because you don't have time to train it. If you think he's worth teaching, start with the basics. Take the responsibility away from him, and show him a good time. If you're looking for someone who already knows how to rock your world in the bedroom, find someone else. And don't worry too much about your boyfriend's imminent future dealing with a fear of intimacy.

I wish I would've spent more time answering this one. It was the first letter I had ever received on that subject, and it certainly was not my last. I quickly wised up and realized my answers to these issues required much more than a moderately snarky paragraph.

If you have the divine privilege of taking your new partner's virginity, the worst thing you can do is have any sort of optimistic expectations. What you can expect is a nervous partner who probably has no idea where to sit or stand or lie down, or what to say, or what to do with his hands. And if your partner knows you have experience, he'll probably be intimidated and worried about meeting the standards he assumes you have already set for him. Your first sexual encounter is generally something you remember for the rest of your life, so it's a good idea to make sure your partner's memory isn't of how bad he was, but rather of how good you were.

For men, the awkwardness of their first time is not exactly the proudest of moments, but the idea of no longer being a virgin usually is. Therefore, if it's the woman who's experienced, I don't recommend being a sex ed. teacher the first time around (unless you can make it kinky, that is). Make it memorable, and start your lesson later. And as for the experienced man who is taking the virginity of his girlfriend – well, that's a book in itself. The main thing for everyone to remember, however, is to be considerate and understanding.

Primarily, inexperience causes conflict among couples because either the experienced person expects satisfaction, or the inexperienced partner is too proud to ask for help. I've heard stories where the boyfriend got extremely upset and emotional after being unable to get an erection during his would-be first sexual encounter. It's difficult to predict how someone will react to being disillusioned about having sex for the first time, so the key is to address the possibilities before you even go that far.

In the situation with "Disappointed," she focused on how bad her boyfriend performed in bed and how *she* felt about that. What she should have done, however, is focus on how *he* feels as the inexperienced one. I'm sure he knows he's bad at sex, but he might not be ready to admit that to someone who doesn't seem willing to be understanding about it. We all need a little bit of gentle guidance every now and then.

This lack of experience is not always about sex, either. Even in college, there are plenty of people who have never had a serious relationship or even a relationship at all. "Disappointed's" boyfriend, for example, never had a girlfriend. While he at least knew how to sweet-talk a girl, he didn't necessarily know some of the other basics, like communication and compromise, let alone how to address the difficult stuff like conflict and commitment. Can you imagine being in his position? Sure you can, because at some point in your life, you *were*.

So quit picking on the newbie and consider the learning experience as just another opportunity for a couple's activity. There will be bumps along the way, and maybe a bit of frustration. But if the connection is there, you can work the rest of it out. You should be the teacher, and your partner can be the naughty student who really, really needs that A in human anatomy class.


## Merry Gift-mas

MATERIAL GOODS, created or bought, are given too much importance in a relationship. Think about how many times a year the average American couple gives presents to each other: Christmas or equivalent, birthdays, Valentine's Day, the anniversary, maybe

Mother's Day and Father's Day, and even Easter sometimes. That doesn't include the random "this made me think of you" gifts we buy for one another throughout the year. Gifts make us feel special, appreciated, and loved by others. Thus, it's only natural that a new couple might try to go all out for Christmas, Valentine's Day, or whatever holiday that approaches their togetherness first. It's a lovely ritual – unless one person didn't get the memo about how much the other person is spending.

Imagine a couple who came together at the end of November. They're happy, basking in New Relationship Syndrome and wanting nothing more than to keep everything just peachy. Luckily, the approaching holiday is perfect for showing just how much they mean to each other – the key words here being "how much."

A couple who has only been together for a month will not be as in tune as a married couple, so it can be difficult to determine what to get each other and even more difficult to determine how much to spend. Let's assume in this scenario that, as full-time students with part-time jobs and government or parental financial assistance, they both have the same Christmas budget of around three hundred dollars (and I'm being generous here. I had far less than that sometimes).

She might be the kind of girl who takes her gift budget and distributes it among many people, spending twenty dollars each on eleven friends and family members, thirty dollars on her best friend, and leaving about fifty dollars for her boyfriend this year. He, on the other hand, budgets his money to spend a hundred dollars on his parents and two hundred dollars on his girlfriend. Or let's imagine in a more extreme case that the guy maxed out a credit card, while she had a very structured budget of twenty dollars per person regardless of who they are. Is this truly an issue to be worried about? I say no.

It's a manufactured problem that causes unnecessary stress among couples. I see people spending too much time figuring out how much their significant others are spending and not enough time figuring out *what* to buy them. Some people go even further than money, stressing about getting the same quantity of items that he got for her, or getting a gift that's in the same league of intimacy (jewelry and perfume vs. movies and gadgets). God forbid he got her a nice bracelet if she bought him three DVDs and a new golf bag. Or even worse, she sticks to that fifty-dollar limit and gets him just two of the three DVDs and no golf bag.

Everyone knows this can happen, so many couples choose to worry about making sure it doesn't. What they fail to realize, however, is that it just doesn't matter.

Here are the reasons people worry about what their significant others bought:

1. Monetary equality – An obvious one; it's the misconception that spending less means you care less, so matching budgets becomes top priority.

2. Quantitative equality – If you heard through the grapevine that he got you seven presents, you feel obligated to get him the same amount of gifts so it doesn't look like you didn't put as much effort into it as he did.

3. Competition – Some people want to establish dominance early in the relationship, and they believe putting the most thought and spending the most money will accomplish that. The key is to outdo him this Christmas, they decide. You could be doing this without realizing it.

4. Appropriateness – It's the fear of being alienated and moving too fast. "Should I get him silk boxers? What if he just got me a CD?"

5. Previous disappointment – I've heard this excuse more than once: "He told me how bad his ex was at giving gifts, so I don't want to mess this up."

I challenge you to completely stop caring about whether your gift is appropriately matching or exceeding the value of what you're buying for your significant other. After all, if that kind of materialism has any real effect on the relationship, you should see a problem with that, and it's probably best that you find out now rather than later down the road when you eventually lose the "what if he got me this?" game. But give each other some credit; it really is the thought that counts.

Having said that, appropriateness (reason 4) is a reason I can understand, but it shouldn't be obsessed about. It's true that an expensive or otherwise over-the-top gift could come across as condescending or a little pushy. And there are the obvious generally-not-a-good-idea gifts for a new relationship, like engagement rings and books of baby names. There are also less obvious ones that can only be determined through observation, but that's your job.

As it gets closer to Christmas or Valentine's Day, I get a lot of questions about whether it's OK to give high-end jewelry to new girlfriends or if a new boyfriend would be turned off by a CD of love songs. Generally, it seems like either would be fine, so long as the jewelry isn't an engagement ring or anything that symbolizes a request for long-term commitment. Same goes for the CD. It's just music, not a frighteningly early confession of your undying love.

But even so, these questions can be difficult to answer because it depends on the type of person you're dating. I know plenty of people who are uncomfortable or even scared to death of receiving gifts that are too personal or too expensive. You might not know what to buy, but you should be familiar with your partner enough to know what *not* to buy.

If mutual spending is such a big deal to you, talking to your significant other certainly isn't out of the question, and it won't take away from the surprise of the gift. Get this conversation out of the way so you'll have more time to come up with a great gift idea.

It's important to avoid setting rules about spending, however. The rules will be broken, and you will feel guilty for staying within the set limits. So, instead of rules, just explain your own spending threshold. Whether you're tight on money or you like to buy gifts for everyone, it might suit you to get that information out in the open. He might be the same way, or he could tell you he doesn't have a lot of people to buy for and plans to spend his budget on you. Or maybe he doesn't want to tell you anything about what he spent or plans to spend because he has a nice surprise in store for you. Ultimately, what you'll probably discover is that your mate doesn't care how much you spend. So why should you?

## *Butterflies Don't Live Very Long*

THE L-WORD, I find, is treated either too loosely or too conservatively. Some couples claim love on day two, and others curl up in a protected ball if their significant other brings up love in the first six months of a relationship.

Sorry, but I don't think there is such a thing as love at first sight, and on the flip side, I know no one wants to wait around for "eventual love."

Love at first sight is when that degrading word "infatuation" comes into play. If you treat the romantic-type love as it's described in the dictionary, two people who have just met cannot possibly be in love – they do not have a "tender, passionate affection" for each other because they've only known each other for several minutes. Or maybe they do. Maybe they are both OK with using the word "love" and treating it how they feel like treating it.

Unfortunately, there are about thirty definitions of love, creating many loopholes for brand new couples who throw around the L-word. Some people feel that the word has lost its power because of this.

The other extreme is worse. When you place too much value on the idea of love, you allow the difficulties of romance and relationships to get the best of you. Imagine a kung fu master who was too judicious about using his skills to defend himself – and similarly, imagine one who kicked anyone who gave him a wrong look.

That's what we have in the world of college romance: a bunch of overzealous kung fu masters kicking other kung fu masters who aren't sure when it's OK to fight back. Society has told us that moving too fast is a bad idea, and moving too slow hints at fear of intimacy, but everyone still chooses an extreme. And it's easy to make your own rules about love – just as easy as it is to say "there are no rules for love." Know why? Because nobody really understands what love is. No one knows *how* to be in love.

In an especially snarky mood, I once wrote an advice column about what love is.

I said, "Love – falling in love – is a 10-year-old boy standing before the tallest, fastest rollercoaster in the world. It's a balance of excitement and fear that human nature craves above all other things. It's a huge book of clichés that you cannot read fast enough. It's intimidating, exhilarating, and completely in control."

My intent was to confuse the daylights out of everyone and get the point across that there is no red flag or alarm for love. Unfortunately, many college students liked my definition and said, "That's *exactly* how I feel about [name]!"

Good, but how do you know it's love?

I found that through my short description of love, I merely reaffirmed couples' feelings and made other couples rethink their level of commitment. The description did no good.

No description of love is good, accurate, useful, or necessary. It's a human emotion that makes relationships work long-term, and I won't tell you when to say it to your partner. I will only tell you to say it if you mean it, and say it the very instant you mean it. Love is not a binding contract, nor is it a tactic for gratification. It's an important word with a couple dozen meanings. Choose one or make one up. Just don't keep your partner in the dark about it.

If you indeed feel like a 10-year-old boy standing in front of a massive amusement park ride, call it something – anything but love.

But if you feel like you're in love, call it love. This is the easy part of the book.

## *Please Stop Groping Each Other*

IT'S KIND of gross, and we're in a church. Ew, are you licking his neck? You do realize people are watching, right? It doesn't bother you that you're being incredibly inconsiderate to those around you?

Well, OK then.

Yes, PDA (Public Display of Affection) is all around us, as rampant as young love, new love, and love that needs public justification. Some couples just want to show off, while others want to prove to the rest of the world that their relationship is the best there ever was. The rest of them just can't keep their hands off their partners.

It's gross to others if you get carried away, and the level of PDA you and your partner wish to show is dependent on how little you care about how it makes other people feel. And it usually irritates others. Some might argue that people who don't like to see a couple kissing, cuddling, and groping each other are just jealous. They may also say that couples who don't show a certain level of affection for each other in public are probably not as happy as the PDA-crazy couple. Of course, none of this is true.

Nowadays, we just *expect* a new couple to engage in a borderline-obscene amount of PDA (See my segment about NRS on page 37). Everything's new and exciting and wonderful and perfect – so they must show everyone how great life can be when you have someone who will gladly put his tongue down your throat at any given moment. But just because we expect it does not mean we abhor it any less. You can call the single folks jealous, but overshadowing that smidgen of jealousy is actually a ton of aggravation for having to be subjected to soft-core porn against their will.

And you can say that other couples just aren't as close or comfortable with each other as you two are, but you know better. Other couples either already went through that PDA stage or they had enough restraint to maintain some humility. The level of public affection a couple engages in has absolutely nothing to do with how happy they are. You have no idea what that couple does together behind closed doors, which is where it really matters.

Of course, not all PDA is bad, but I hesitate to call it PDA because it's mostly normal. It's all about intensity vs. location. I don't consider it disturbing to anyone if you sit close together in class, as long as you are paying attention and not kissing, cuddling, or holding hands.

In a date setting in public, the occasional touch and light kiss can go a long way to set the mood, though I would hope a couple could show good judgment in the presence of children or people who are just trying to go about their daily business (i.e. A mall is for shopping, not dry-humping). At a party with friends, it's perfectly fine to sit close together, hold hands, and even steal a kiss every now and then; you don't need to do anything else to send the signal that you and your partner are a couple (though I suppose if everyone is busy making out, you might as well fit in).

But if you're at the movies, you damn well better be sitting still and watching the movie.

This is just my opinion, however (and likely the opinion of most everyone else), and some people smile when they see PDA anywhere because they know the couple is happy. Ultimately, a couple will do what they want to do, and if it upsets the rest of us, then so be it. We'll get over it. Just don't do it for the sake of proving anything to the public; do it because you really want to make out or cuddle.

While we do get to make our own decisions about being lovey-dovey in public (in certain locations, mind you. There are many places, including campuses, that ban PDA), sometimes the couple doesn't agree on what is appropriate.

Scenario: Your boyfriend has no problem hanging all over you and making out in front of everyone, but other people's PDA really bothers you, and you'd rather not be *that* couple. You and your partner's respective opinions might be on opposite extremes, which makes it difficult to appear functional in public. You're always pushing his hand away, and he keeps trying to steal kisses. To strangers, it might look like you're mad at him, and all he wants is a little bit of attention in public.

PDA is difficult to compromise. I'm more in favor of bending toward the person opposed to it. Instead of the anti-PDA partner meeting halfway, he should meet more like twenty-five percent of the way – or maybe even ten percent of the way. And only if he's willing.

I know this sounds awfully conservative of me, and I do apologize, but I just can't suggest an equal PDA compromise when it has more potential to weaken a relationship rather than strengthen it. If your partner doesn't advocate PDA, inflicting any amount of it on him will create too much tension. Imagine how you feel when a complete stranger hugs you for more than six or seven seconds; that's how your partner feels when you show him affection in public when he doesn't want it. In the end, though, you might get him to tolerate it; I hope you enjoy the conflict this will inevitably create.

Showing affection in public is not the worst thing a couple can do, and while people like me will gag, tell you to get a room, and wonder whether your grope-fest is just a façade for deeper problems, it's always up to the *couple* whether or not it's appropriate. If your partner simply cannot stand PDA, you have to accept that and stop trying to force the issue. He might change his mind one day, or he might not. Either way, his unwillingness to make out with you or even hug you in public has nothing to do with being insecure. If you can't come to terms with that, think about why putting a portion of your physical relationship on display is so important to *you*.

## *Embarrassed, Snookum-Cakes?*

WE LOVE our sweeties, honeys, pumpkins, snookumses, gumdrops, sugars, babies, honey bears, snuggle fucks, love dumplings, baby dolls, boos, bunnies, and kitten puffs. These pet names for our partners can develop early in the relationship and become so commonplace that it seems awkward to call your partner by his actual name.

The general consensus seems to be that couples who use pet names in public are irritating, especially if the names are something outlandish like "Big Warm Daddy Bear" or "Snuggles McPuffaluff" (Yes, I just kind of pulled those from thin air). So, knowing this, we will try to be considerate of others when talking to our partners in public. Some couples who insist on pet names no matter what might even develop "public" pet names – typical ones like Hun, Honey, Sweetie, or Baby. But behind closed doors it's Cuddle Kitten, Daddy Sugars, and Slurpy Bottoms. Some people have no shame and will call their mate whatever they want, anytime they want. Others are just too embarrassed to admit to even having pet names for each other, let alone having those cutesy code words for sex and their partner's genitals.

Couples have asked me if it's OK to be weird and use odd pet names or have odd little quirks and rituals. Stereotypes suggest that couples who baby-talk each other all the time are disgustingly sheltered, and those who are in love don't need to front it so blatantly. And then people become reluctant to have any sort of uniqueness to their relationship because of how stupid that other couple in the bookstore looked.

But the question should not be whether it's OK to be weird, because it's not weird. Nothing should be considered "weird" except to an outsider. The fact is, most couples have pet names, rituals, quirks, and habits that seem unbelievably kooky to everyone else. The majority of us are either too embarrassed to admit it, or we just don't think anyone else cares.

If you are embarrassed about what you and your significant

other do in private, consider this your invitation to get it out in the open. You can be proud of being weird, or you can be proud that weird is normal. Either one is correct.

Obviously, I'm not saying you should tell anyone all about the little private things you do behind closed doors. You probably don't care to tell your friends about you and your partner's weekly nurse-patient role-playing or that you like to wear her clothes every third Saturday. I doubt a lot of people would admit to their regular S&M sessions, either.

Not that every couple does stuff *that* abnormal. Several couples have shared their quirks with me, and some of them are quite common. For example, new couples love to celebrate the "monthiversary," doing something special each month they've been together. One couple, who had been together three years at the time of this writing, drinks a glass of a certain wine, because it was what they were both drinking when they first met. Other couples had admitted to trying new things in the bedroom on their monthiversary celebrations. I certainly wouldn't call these traditions weird.

I've heard of couples who, on their anniversary, try to have sex once for every year they've been together. I can imagine that becomes more difficult the longer you've been together and the older you get.

You might not care to admit even the mildest of quirks to your friends, but you shouldn't ridicule people who do decide to be open about it (but by all means, feel free to ask them to shut up). If you don't have something similar that you and your partner share, maybe you're the one who should be ridiculed.

Your relationship is not doomed if by some chance you don't have anything unique or weird you share with your partner. As long as you haven't been avoiding the advent of these rituals on the basis that you don't think they are normal, then you're probably in a normal relationship yourself. Don't feel obligated to change anything, especially without your partner's knowledge. The real problem with couple quirks arises when one person wants it and the other does not, or when one person doesn't take it as seriously as the other does.

The bond brought on by a couple's uniqueness can only be shared if both partners have mutually agreed upon a ritual, pet name, or quirk. One person cannot manufacture a ritual and expect it to be set in stone. If your partner is adamant on incorporating a new ritual into the mix, treat it like you would treat an odd fetish your partner might have: Compromise.

If you want a really ridiculous example, a couple who had been together two years got in a fight one day about something that seemed trivial to you and me but was very important to at least one person in that relationship. Several months prior, they were making fun of a movie trailer they saw on TV. Based on how terrible the film looked, both of them said they did not want to see it.

Well, one day the boyfriend ended up watching the movie at a friend's apartment. It wasn't a planned event, and it wasn't his idea to watch the movie. He called his girlfriend later to tell her that the movie actually wasn't as bad as it looked. And she got upset. Her reasoning was that even though the situation involved something as minor as a movie, it was the spoken agreement to "boycott" the movie that made it such a big deal. He had gone against that bond and saw the movie without consulting her first. It was something they had done as a couple, and she believes he should not have gone outside that boundary. And as for the boyfriend's reasoning – well, he was just confused.

And I hope you aren't surprised that I have to side with the boyfriend on this one. While they may have "agreed" not to see the movie, the importance of this agreement is all but nonexistent. The girlfriend wanted it to be something special, but this was really just an attempt to manufacture uniqueness in a relationship. Her snookum-cakes saw a movie she didn't want to see. If she has an issue with that, it seems like she's holding on to any shred of security she can find; they, as a couple, should find out why.

Overall, the point of this segment is to convey that nothing is bizarre in a relationship if you both willingly do it together. But if you break out the whips and handcuffs three years down the line and start calling your partner Little Bunny Tits, you might not get your way, and you have to be OK with that.

## *Compromise Time Together*

EVEN IF you think your new significant other is everything you ever wanted, it won't be that way for long. You might not be too excited once you learn about his poker night, his drinking habits, or his weekly flag football tournament. I could throw more stereotypes your way, but you get it.

If you can make it to the long-term commitment stage of your relationship, those late-night outings and living habits become even more prominent and more irritating. What happened to the seemingly perfect match sitting across from you at dinner all those nights?

That's when you have to face the facts; your "perfect match" is still there – in all his flawed glory – and that's just how it should be. Unless, of course, you want someone exactly like you.

The truth is, your lives are going to clash, and so will your romance if you let it. Before you take anything further, it's time to compromise.

Relationship compromising is not the same as one person bending toward the other because the other made a better argument. It's not the same as giving your partner an ultimatum. Once you're already in the relationship, compromise must be equal sacrifice, because entering a relationship with someone means you've agreed to equal partnership. As two college students with similar ambition and lofty goals, neither of you will be submissive for very long.

Compromise is mostly about working around your current lives to give each other an entry point to share experiences. Relationships function best when people can turn personal enjoyment into couple enjoyment and turn personal friends into mutual friends. In short, don't exclude your partner from your regular activities.

But that's the best-case scenario, not practical advice. Not every couple can easily integrate themselves into each other's lives, either because it's not practical or it's not interesting. If you're OK with keeping activities and friends separate, your ultimate goal will be to keep a balance and make sure both of you are happy. Here are a few tips:

1. No sacrifices – Your partner should not have to sacrifice any activities he's been previously doing, and neither should you. If they are cutting into alone time, it's up to both of you to willingly and mutually agree on exclusive days to be alone.

2. Equality – If you think a so-called compromise is more beneficial to your partner than it is for you, address it like an adult. If you get hostile or whiney, you appear as the one who wants the most out of the deal.

3. No ultimatums – If you are the stay-at-home type and he is the going-out type, just accept it as part of his personality. Don't withhold affection just because he made previous plans with his friends and won't cancel them. Remind yourself that you have cho-

sen a partner who has a certain way of life. He is likely just as perturbed that you won't go out with him as you are that he won't stay home with you.

4. Some compromises shouldn't exist – If your partner is constantly planning outings to which you are not invited, there is no excuse for that. Relationships take work, and putting time into it is part of the job. Your partner might have been used to going out with his friends every weekend, but now there needs to be balance. If you aren't invited, there should be a valid reason and an effort to make time for you in other ways.

5. Alone time is real time – Lastly, being invited out with your partner's friends is one thing, but it doesn't hold a candle to being alone together. Alone time is what really counts as quality time together, and it should be something both of you want more often than not.

Those last two are actually serious issues in many relationships, and it seems that men are the primary culprits. I've probably received half a dozen letters about this problem during my short time as an actual advice columnist. The following letter is a good example of compromise gone wrong:

*Dear Stephen,*

*My boyfriend and I have been together for about two months, and I've already noticed a trend. He likes to see his friends more than he likes to see me. Even when we are together, we are out at a bar with his friends. We are in his apartment with his friends. We are in the pool with his friends. We've been alone together ex-*

*actly twice in two months. Every other time, at least one friend of his has been around. I'm getting to the point where I just want to jump on my boyfriend and get down to business, no matter who watches.*

*I asked him why he does this and he just said he likes to show me off to his friends. We had a huge argument about it once, and it just ended in me giving up and him thinking he was right. Well, I am getting impatient. What can I do to get him alone more often?*

*- Annoyed*

Good question, "Annoyed." Why would your new boyfriend continue to favor being around his friends when he has something new and exciting right in front of him? It could be one of several reasons, like fear of intimacy, low self-esteem, and inexperience. So, "Annoyed" has two options as far I'm concerned: (1) She can make it clear to her boyfriend that balancing their "out" time and "alone" time must be done immediately without fail; to help this along, they can have a long conversation about priorities, what it takes to maintain a healthy relationship, and what could be inhibiting their progress as a couple – or (2) She can end it.

Taking the first route is commendable and could make things run smoothly in the long run, but the second route is the practical option. Throughout this book I harp on the fact that couples are often too quick to end salvageable relationships, but get one thing straight: A new relationship is like a new car; if there are serious problems, get another one immediately. In this situation, I consider the fruitless argument a red flag.

Compromising in the beginning will be difficult because new couples are afraid to address problems so soon in the relationship. But it can't be neglected, and it can't be resisted. If such an attempt to compromise is faced with any resistance in the beginning, it will get exponentially worse as time goes on. Test the waters *now*.

# 3

# The Outside

Relationships would have a higher success rate if everyone could keep the doors of their minds open only to their partners and be in control of their love lives without the influence of others. In fact, many couples have successfully managed to do just that, but most of us find it difficult. We are very much involved with the actions and voices of friends, family, and other couples, and we can't help but let it affect our decisions.

We quietly judge each other every day, and some of us even aspire to mimic the actions and ideals of those we admire. This extends to our love lives, where some people are insecure about whether they are on the right track.

Couples often seek approval and insight from those who appear knowledgeable or stable. But even the couples who try to keep to themselves will end up being on the receiving end of unsolicited opinions. Being too open to what other people think can destroy an otherwise "normal" relationship.

However, outside influence is not limited to other opinions, as you will find in this chapter. Here, you will read about "the outside" and how it influences couples. Do the parents not approve of your relationship? Is there an ex who's still in the picture? Does it drive you crazy to see him look at another woman? Can you not get a single moment of privacy because people are *always* around? Does your love interest have a child?

The relationship is yours, so learn how to treat it as such.

# *Parental Disapproval*

TRADITIONALLY raised children grow up with the constant desire to make their parents proud, or at least avoid punishment. But the teen years tend to bring blatant rebellion, and by the time we are adults, we take our parents' views into consideration but ultimately make our own decisions.

Dating opportunities can be limited for a teenager if the child's parents don't approve of the date. In stereotypical cases of disapproval, a teen girl might want to date an older man with some sort of "bad boy" aspect about him – a motorcycle, a piercing or eight, tattoos, unemployed, and so on. Under the worst circumstances, a teenager will actually run away with her romantic interest, making it a big ordeal. In 2005, for example, a 16-year-old girl from Michigan named Katherine Lester fled to the Middle East to be with a 20-year-old Palestinian man she met on MySpace.com.

But in typical circumstances, the infatuation goes away or the parents cut the child some slack. Well-informed parents will know when to keep their mouths shut and let the relationship end without inciting rebellion. Of course, that doesn't apply to anything illegal.

Other cases of parental disapproval include interracial and homosexual relationships, which, for good parents, can be much easier to accept than a jobless 22-year-old who wants to "woo" their teen daughter. Homosexuality is not a choice, and interracial relationships are still relationships; both are a non-issue – unless the love interest in question is 22 years old, drives a motorcycle, and doesn't have a job.

By the time we hit our college years, most of us are capable of looking after our own best interests, as long as we were raised right. When it comes to dating as an adult, we're either gay or we aren't; we're either dating someone of a different ethnicity or we aren't. Our lives, our decisions. We have finally decided to let go of those who don't accept us, and we simply move forward.

Still, not everyone is so confident and hard-shelled. There are those who maintain a strong attachment to home and family even after moving out – and of course, there are plenty of college students who remain financially dependent on their parents for several years. So it kind of matters who they bring home for the holidays.

A white woman in her mid-20s married her black boyfriend after they both graduated. Her parents did not attend the wedding, as they had disowned her and cut her off financially several years prior, after she first introduced the black boyfriend to the family. Last I heard, they were doing quite well. Happy and successful – she knew it would work out and did not let anything stop her from continuing to be happy.

Similarly, a Catholic married his atheist girlfriend, and his very religious parents never forgave him. They've been married for fifteen years. This couple didn't let their parents' ideals stop them from embracing their own.

I hope you enjoyed those two mini-stories of triumph over adversity, but don't consider them an excuse to make a bad decision. These stories could have gone differently. The couples were just like any other couple, and their defiant love is not immune to failure. The interracial couple could get a divorce one day, as could the atheist and the Catholic – the same applies to two Baptists, two Jews, two black people, two white people, two gay people, a Satanist and a Buddhist, or two hermaphrodites. That's the way love works: You're in it, then you're out of it, or you're not in it from the start – or you're always in it. Love requires risk.

Yes, I'm telling you that as an adult, you should treat relationships your parents disapprove of the same as you would treat relationships your parents strongly advocate. My reasoning is that your parents either raised you well or they didn't. If they did, you are all set to make educated decisions about what kind of person is right for you. But if your upbringing has rendered you incapable of making the right choice, it certainly shouldn't be your parents who tell you how to make that decision now. If they couldn't instill good judgment when you were an impressionable child, don't sacrifice something so important just to give them a second chance.

Imagine if the Catholic and the white woman had listened to their parents and never married their respective significant others (the atheist woman and the black man). After eventually moving on and finding someone "suitable" in the eyes of their parents, they'll end up in a potentially half-hearted marriage with imminent divorce. Or perhaps not; if they were willing to give up the old relationship for the sake of parental approval, was it really that strong of a bond? We know who's qualified to make that decision.

Obviously, race and religion are not reasons to end a relationship unless they cause conflict among the couple (for example, forcing views and culture on your partner), and sexuality is not something to be controlled by anyone. But even if your parents merely disapprove of your significant other's character, your educated judgment still prevails.

And those are my words of encouragement. Before you tell Mom and Dad to shove off, however, keep reading.

The previous advice is for adults, not teenagers. I feel I must qualify everything I said with a disclaimer because I remember being a teen and taking only the advice I wanted to hear. Being told he is smart enough to make his own decisions is wonderful news for a teen, but it's not the truth. Teenagers are not adults, and they are not yet qualified to refer to their decisions as "adult" ones. If you're a child dating an adult high-school dropout, "love" becomes irrelevant.

When Katherine Lester turned 18, she went back to the Middle East, since, as an adult, she could do this without parental consent. She wasn't gone two months. Katherine ended up dumping that MySpace man on a November 2007 airing of *Dr. Phil*. It turned out that her dream-guy was possessive and verbally abusive.

I could fill up a book with all of the stupid things teenagers do in relationships, but I'll leave that up to the rest of the world. Bottom line: Typically, teens aren't ready to make a logical decision about love.

I have one final caveat for the rest of you. This section mentions a lot about parental disapproval of your significant others based on race and religion, where the decision to ignore your parents is an easy one. But, of course, it isn't necessarily always the problem. You can't discount your Baptist parents just because they don't like your Jewish boyfriend. It's easy to brush aside disagreeable opinions and label them as prejudiced, but it takes real maturity to consider the potential of deeper concerns. Katherine Lester's parents were quite disapproving of their daughter's decision to run away to Israel's West Bank, one of the most *dangerous* parts of the world, to be with that 20-year-old man. Do you think it was just because of his religion?

While the decision on who you date is still yours, make sure you aren't missing something major about him that your parents were able to see.

Like, for example, a police sketch on TV.

## *Cut The Rope*

MEET "BRITTANY," a 19-year-old sophomore who started dating a guy she met at a bar one night. At the risk of attaching a stigma to the bar-going type, her new boyfriend – we'll call him "Paul" – was the partying type, while Brittany was only out that night because it was her friend's birthday.

There were plenty more little social differences they had, but the point of this mild example is to talk about Brittany's friends. They didn't approve of Paul; they thought she was too good for him. She argued they were wrong. They didn't interfere. She dated Paul for a while and eventually realized the relationship couldn't work, and they broke up. They were just too different, and her friends saw that in the beginning.

But she did well not to listen. Just because the relationship ended does not mean she should have gone with outside advice from biased people. And that's what I primarily preach to couples about outside influence. Make your own decisions; nothing else matters. This *book* doesn't even matter. If you disagree with any of my views, don't make them part of your lifestyle and decision-making. Like all good advice, my words are meant to guide, empower, and inspire decisions which are ultimately yours. If you ever get advice that leaves you without options, create the option to ignore it.

Brittany could have listened to her friends' advice about Paul. They would've been right, and she would not have wasted her time with him. What about the next guy? If she decided to listen to her friends, she would probably avoid all men who seemed to be incompatible with her on the surface – or worse, she might present every new guy to her friends to get the green light.

It's a sad thing to see people putting too much trust in others and neglecting the benefit of personal experience. Brittany, fortunately, was able to see her relationship with Paul through to the end. As a result, she learned and grew and experienced and taught and lived and loved. Had she taken the route of listening to her friends, she would have simply followed.

Brittany has no idea who she will end up marrying one day, but she knows she wants to get married. For her to get to that point, she will have to learn what she wants and needs from a significant other. She will have to decide what works and what doesn't. Listening to a friend's advice about who to date is counterproductive to her ultimate goal.

This brings to mind a terrible song by Avril Lavigne called "Sk8er Boi" – or "Skater Boy" for those of you who prefer adult English. It's about a girl who turned down a date with a "punk" boy because her friends did not approve of his unconventional lifestyle. The song teaches the lesson to be true to yourself – I think. Had the girl gone with her initial feelings, she would've ended up with a successful rock star. Instead, she became a single mom. Despite how ridiculous this song is, we can derive one thing: Had she given the "punk" a chance, she may or may *not* have become a lonely single mom. Why would you allow a friend to dictate whether or not that happens?

If you aren't being abused or otherwise mistreated by your new partner, your true friends will appreciate that you want to give the relationship a try. They will still tell you they disapprove, and they will try to convince you to find someone "better," but they will never go any further than that. You shouldn't *allow* them to go any further than that. There are a few safe rules that will prevent a friend from crossing that line between offering an opinion and flat-out meddling.

Rule number one, expect advice. She's your friend for a reason. You should be receptive of her opinion, and vice versa. Allow her to say her peace. She likes him, she hates him – whatever.

Number two, respectfully explain your position on the matter. Hostility or accusations will tell your friend that she isn't important to your life anymore. Instead, ask her for support in making your new relationship a learning experience. Tell her you respect her opinion, and you would like her to be there for you if it doesn't work out.

Number three, ignore the I-told-you-sos. If it ends, a real friend will comfort you, but even a best friend will be tempted to slip in one or two comments about being right. Remember that it's better you know she's right rather than wonder if she could've been wrong. It's all part of personal growth, and it's one step further to knowing how to make a relationship work in the long run.

Number four, if you see evidence of your friend interfering with your relationship, break contact immediately and forewarn your partner. Make sure he tells you if your friend makes contact with him. If you passively allow it to continue, you aren't standing up for your right to make your own decisions about dating. It's hard for someone to respect that.

And finally, there is no right time to openly gloat about the relationship succeeding. Even ten years down the road, when you're married and pregnant with your second child, you should simply be satisfied with yourself that you made it work without outside help. Don't resent your friend for trying to discourage you from dating him; instead, thank her for ultimately being supportive and not interfering.

Overall, friends want what's best for you, but they can accept that your freedom of choice is what's really best. Remind your friends about the importance of mutual respect. Remind yourself that sometimes, when we attempt to progress, a figurative rope is attached, pulling us back and keeping us from going forward. Cut the rope; it's not a chain.

## *'Meet My Ex'*

THE EX is not usually someone we want to hear about, let alone meet. As far as we are concerned, your ex is your ex and is such for a good reason. But sometimes breakups are genuinely clean and mutual, and staying friends is easy; just because it didn't work out romantically doesn't mean you have nothing in common.

This makes a new significant other uncomfortable most of the time, whether he admits it or not. It is, however, something people can tolerate and deal with – as long as the ex doesn't make any of the following mistakes:

1. Offering advice or consolation – Something obviously prevented the ex and your partner from staying together, so what gives her the right to be the shoulder to cry on or the therapist for your relationship? It's not her business, and she doesn't want to know what will happen if she ever makes it her business.

2. Flirt – It's over between them. They had their chance to flirt and do much more than that, but not anymore. If the ex flirts with your partner, it's a serious sign of disrespect, whether the flirting is harmless or not.

3. Hang out alone – Again, that time has passed. Friends or not, an ex needs supervision. It's inappropriate for the ex and your partner to meet in a private setting, or even have dinner together without talking to you about it first.

4. Talk down to you – If an ex talks down to you, it's another sign of disrespect. If she doesn't respect you, she probably won't be above taking matters into her own hands to dictate how your relationship plays out – and how it eventually ends.

5. Compete with you – If she thinks she looks better, treated him better, or pleased him better, she damn well better keep it to

herself. They aren't together anymore, so at least one person has moved on. You hope.

But it's not all up to the ex, of course. For those of you who are still friends with your ex, it's more important what *you* do to prevent your partner from being uncomfortable about the situation.

First of all, confiding in the ex is off limits. If you're close friends with your ex, it might seem tempting to ask for input about dealing with something your partner did to upset you. Whether you realize it or not, your ex's advice will probably be too biased. Ask someone else.

Flirting is a two-way street, and so is being alone together. If the ex flirts, ignore it and discourage it in the future. Make it clear to your ex that you wish to respect your partner's position on the matter. No hanging out alone, no reminiscing about old times, and not even the slightest bit of flirting.

In the event that the ex and your partner get in a competition, remember who you're dating. I don't care if the ex could get your rocks off like no one else; that's only for you to know. Take your partner's side. Always. If you don't, then you are more at fault than the ex.

Defend your partner under all circumstances. And let your ex know one thing: If he can't respect that you've moved on, he isn't a friend in any sense.

These guidelines might seem a bit strict and paranoid to some of you, but it reflects how most people feel about their partners' exes. The aforementioned points are the ideal rules for interacting with exes, though I realize not every couple feels this way. Some are more lax about what their partners do with their exes. However, in such cases, you have to make sure your partner is *really* OK with it and that it's not just an issue of tolerance. Eventually, that tolerance will be stretched beyond its tensile strength.

Here are a few more guidelines to make sure you can both agree on an appropriate level of interaction with an ex:

1. Trust – If you're uneasy about your partner interacting with his ex, try to trust him and hope he doesn't let you down. I know you might say it's the ex you don't trust, but realize that it will take just as much effort from your partner to allow anything to happen. If he cheats on you, there are no excuses.

2. Communicate – If you plan to meet with your ex, make sure your partner knows about it under all circumstances. Even if it was a last-minute thing, call him and at least leave a voice message. If you bump into the ex at a coffee shop and sit down for a chat, tell your partner either with a text message during the conversation or a phone call soon after. If your partner is constantly in the know, there will be less reason for suspicion.

3. Set fair guidelines – Never do anything with your ex that you know will make your partner uncomfortable. Don't cancel plans with your partner to make plans with your ex. In fact, it's advisable to put your partner first even if you had prior plans with the ex. Your ex shouldn't have an all-access pass to your life and your private time; he shouldn't be allowed to call you "just to chat" when he knows you're with your partner. If he's calling you more than a couple of times a week, it's probably a good idea to enforce boundaries. Your partner should never have to compete with the ex for your time.

4. Constantly reassure – Tell him he's numero uno in your life. Ask for his advice about being friends with your ex. Be open and honest about it. Let him know that you don't have any feelings for your ex but that you think they can at least stay friends, but tell your partner that you care more about his opinion and will respect

his wishes. Ultimately, that is what you will have to do if you want him to make any sort of long-term commitment with you.

5. Encourage them to meet – If your ex is dating someone, ask your partner about a double date. If your ex is still single, invite him to have coffee with you and your partner in a neutral setting. In either case, avoid alcohol on the first meeting. You'll want everyone to be able to filter their thoughts.

Above all, compromise is important. We can't expect our significant others to break all contact with their exes just because we aren't comfortable with it, but you should also realize there are certain lines you can't cross, and you and your partner must draw them together.

## *The Double Date*

THERE'S NOTHING that can bring conflict to a happy couple more than another couple. People love to compare their relationships to other ones, but as a result, they often make the mistake of desiring more from their significant others, even if they've been happy all this time. The double date is prime time for each couple to put on a performance for the other, and that's when things can go sour. The other guy might pull out his girlfriend's chair at dinner and open the car door for her. His girlfriend might allow him to smoke cigars in the house and stay out all night without calling. He sent her flowers before the date and sang her a love song, and she plans to cook him a huge dinner tomorrow.

Not that either of them would say those things to the other couple outright during the double date, but they might try to work it in somehow. And believe me; the other couple is taking notes – material for tomorrow's discussion that will probably escalate into a fight. If the couple has learned how to compromise, the conflict might end well, where both parties have agreed to try to be more like their friends. But why?

Relationship experts will probably agree across the board that a couple who tries to mirror other couples will ultimately end up unhappy, as such an act is a sign of weakness in the relationship. That could be true, but it could also signify a lack of experience – a "we don't know how to act, so let's see what Jack and Betty do" kind of approach. In any case, let's agree that mimicking the relationship habits of others is not advisable in most cases.

A double date is a social gathering, a public appearance so to speak, but it can sometimes turn into a subtle competition. New couples love to show off in public; it's the most common form of reinforcing the attraction and showing everyone else that they are, indeed, in a relationship. New couples are just so darned happy. Sometimes that doesn't transfer well to the established couple across the table. However, it can also go either way – an established couple who lives together, does everything as a team, and knows each other inside and out might cause jealousy in the new couple who wants to fit in like a 16-year-old at a college party.

I have received quite a few letters on this subject, most of them complaining about boyfriends and girlfriends who don't measure up to what seems to be society's standards. Some of the people who wrote in actually admitted to being happy – "until that double date last week." What the hell happened on that double date to suck out all the happiness?

Well, one woman – we'll call her "Kelly" – said the other guy respected his girlfriend's views about alcohol; in other words, he gave up drinking for her. But it had been months since Kelly had a long talk with her boyfriend, "Ben," about drinking. Kelly was against alcohol for religious reasons, while Ben was raised to drink responsibly. Ben, being the good guy he is, tried to quit drinking for her, but he didn't want to give up a social activity based on someone else's beliefs, especially since he was never irresponsible with alcohol.

They reached a compromise; Ben could drink whenever he wanted, but he could not get drunk in front of Kelly, and he most certainly could not drunk-dial her. It's a fine compromise that Ben seemed to have no problem respecting. But Kelly now questions the compromise. Why should she have to "lower" her "standards" when other men seem to respect the ideals of their girlfriends?

There are several problems with this logic. First, there's no guarantee that the other girl's boyfriend will continue to not drink – or even that he's telling the truth. Then there's the issue of how this other guy feels about alcohol. If he never saw drinking as necessary for any occasion, while Ben might be a connoisseur, it's impossible to compare the two boyfriends. Kelly disapproves of alcohol based on her religion, but what about the other girl? She could have a family of alcoholics with whom she is forced to socialize during the holidays – half a dozen drunk, obnoxious family members who have abused and emotionally scarred her since childhood. Hell, maybe the smell of booze makes her violently ill.

Just so it doesn't sound like I'm accusing women of being the sole culprits, here's another example: I received a letter from a guy who felt he was getting "shafted" by compromising with his girl-friend. Months before that dreaded double date that ruined it all, "Gary" moved in with his girlfriend "Sarah." When deciding on chore responsibilities, they agreed to the "I cook, you clean" pol-icy. But on that double date of doom, Gary learned that the other couple had a "*she* cooks, *she* cleans" policy, while the boyfriend's job was to do any outside or mechanical work that needed to be done – a traditional household indeed.

Gary didn't see why he had to be in the kitchen at all, since other couples apparently didn't have a problem with the traditional approach. Again, faulty logic. Upon further questioning, I learned that Gary and his girlfriend live in a one-bedroom apartment. What, pray tell, would be Gary's share of the chores in this "traditional" household?

No couple is exactly the same. Kelly and Ben have their own standards, beliefs, and agreements. They are a couple like Sarah and Gary, who also have their own ways of doing things, and creating a uniform standard by which both of these couples should live would be absurd. So, why should they adhere to the standards of any *other* couple?

If that concept seems even remotely plausible, why stop at that? Maybe everyone should get married exactly two years after the relationship starts and move in six months prior to that. We should all have two children, one dog, and one hamster. The man should work full-time and mow the lawn once a week, while the woman raises the children – and cooks and cleans and feeds the pets and does the laundry. The man should drink Scotch in his study every evening, and the woman is allowed one glass of wine per day. They should agree to have sex at least three times a week, and the man should convert to whatever religion his wife is.

I could go on, but you get the point.

Double dates are going to happen to most couples sooner or later, so we might as well make the best of them. Take the opportunity to observe, enjoy, and appreciate your relationship. The other couple will silently judge you, as you will silently judge them. If it makes you uncomfortable to know this, there's probably something you need to address in your own relationship. This can only be addressed to your significant other, as you two are the only people who can decide how happy you are.

Internal happiness trumps performance. That couple squeezed together on one side of the table could be better or worse than the other. It could be older or newer, strained or comfortable, sexual or emotional, serious or fickle, abusive or romantic. Et cetera. Et cetera. Stop caring, stop comparing.

## *Behold The Super-Couple*

MY FAVORITE television series as a child was *Boy Meets World*. Ah, good old Cory and Topanga. They were living (er, fictional) proof that childhood crushes could blossom into romance, and high-school sweethearts *do* have a chance. And with a connection as strong as theirs, nothing could ever tear them apart for long. If they couldn't last, god help the rest of us.

Cory and Topanga embody the definition of a "Super-Couple." It's a word a select few use to describe the type of couple that somehow becomes the standard for which other couples should function. Many people view a Super-Couple as one who appears absolutely perfect, like Mike and Carol Brady or Ward and June Cleaver.

If you've ever seen what some might call a Super-Couple, you probably noticed how they always seem to do everything together and agree on everything…together – together, together, together. The Super-Couple has been *together* for years, or it sure as hell seems like it. They are practically married, and they even talk like a married couple. What's worse is that they are still lovey-dovey with each other in public after all those years of being with the same person. My word, is there *anything* wrong with them?

And that's when other couples fall into the trap; they admire the Super-Couple to the point that every other couple's success is contingent upon what happens to the Super-Couple in the long run. If it doesn't work out with the Super-Couple, what hope does anyone else have? The high divorce rate in the United States makes it easy to get discouraged about long-term romance. After comparing yourselves to a couple who seems to have no problems, you conclude that their relationship is just infallible, and your romances, past or present, can't measure up to that.

For a good example, I can relate back to *Boy Meets World*, when young Super-Couple Corey and Topanga went through a devastating breakup after Topanga's parents announced their divorce. In Topanga's eyes, her parents, Jedediah and Rhiannon (Or was it Chloe?), had a love that no one else in the world could come close to mirroring. As a result, Topanga indefinitely postponed her wedding.

It was obvious that Jedediah and Rhiannon were a Super-Couple to Topanga, and she made the mistake of basing the feasibility of love on the success of her parents.

I know of at least one person outside of TV who actually ended her relationship when a couple she had looked up to dearly broke it off after more than five years. That's not the norm, obviously. Usually, the couple who previously idolized the now-parted Super-Couple won't completely give up hope. But it does bring unnecessary negativity into their relationship. Someone becomes skeptical about being able to sustain anything long-term, and if and when the opportunity for commitment presents itself, it will be ignored because someone is scared to death of failing. After all, the Super-Couple couldn't make it in this cruel, loveless world. So no one can.

Do any of these idolizing couples ever bother to find out *why* the Super-Couple broke up?

Being a Super-Couple has nothing to do with being "perfect," never fighting, or appearing incredibly romantic even on rainy days. It has nothing to do with being better or more successful than other relationships. What makes a Super-Couple so "Super" is that they know how to perform. No, I'm not saying that all Super-Couples are just dysfunctional relationships in disguise. It's quite the contrary, actually. Many couples are able to hide conflict in the presence of others and deal with it maturely and properly. They don't want to bother the general public with their arguments or issues, and they sure as hell don't want to be judged. They live a life of peace and, best of all, normalcy. And I suppose that's what makes them a Super-Couple, until they break up.

To other couples, such a performance can be perceived as one of two extremes: Either it's a performance to hide serious, deep conflict, or it's simply perfection. It's usually neither, however, and most couples don't realize that everyone puts on a performance to hide at least a little bit of imperfection. Thus, it almost appears that "good" couples never fight – not that any of us believe that for one second. But it's a nice thought.

So, why would a Super-Couple break up? Well, if we're going with the traditional definition of a Super-Couple, they would not break up at all. There are far less of these so-called "Super-Couples" than people think, because when that Super-Couple breaks up, they weren't really such a thing to begin with, or at least they aren't anymore. They had problems just like the rest of us, but maybe they weren't able to resolve them in the end. Maybe it was not technically a "problem," as sometimes people just grow apart and decide it's best to break it off – but that's certainly not Super-Couple material.

In the case of Topanga's parents, Jedediah left his wife for another woman, rendering this "Super-Couple" nonexistent. The true definition of a Super-Couple still lies with my initial example, Corey and Topanga. While some of their problems were evident to the public (and they were big issues sometimes, as per TV show drama demands), they were still able to solve them, and they still loved each other. If you want to believe in the Super-Couple, that's all the definition you need.

I hope that by mentioning the term "Super-Couple" more than twenty times in this segment, you have become disgusted and decided that it is not welcome in your vocabulary. The Super-Couple might exist, but you have far too much work to do in your own relationship to worry about them.

## *Look, But Don't Touch*

ON RARE occasions, the topic of an afternoon talk show will intrigue me. In such a case, the host was addressing the issue of looking at other men and women outside a relationship. Is it OK to look, but don't touch? And is pornography acceptable?

The show featured a young married couple, and the wife was absolutely appalled that her husband not only looked at porn, but he also ogled other women in public – at the mall, at the grocery store, or on the street – in front of his wife. And we're not talking about a sly glance, but rather a more obvious "look at the tits on that one" kind of approach. Of course, the wife argued that her husband should only be looking at her. She said a man should only find his wife attractive; otherwise, he's essentially cheating.

On the flip side, the husband argued that "boys will be boys." He has a right to at least look, he said. He rebutted his wife by saying it's not cheating if he doesn't act on his observations. He went on to explain to the audience that he sometimes intentionally points out hot women in front of his wife just to irk her.

A lot of people might be siding with the wife at this point, especially given that her husband is doing it to piss her off. After all, how can you defend a man who has admitted he habitually does something out of spite for his wife? But, perhaps not all is wrong on his side.

Every couple has their own views about what's acceptable and what's over the line. My opinion on it varies greatly, depending on the situation. For example, I don't think looking at pornography is OK unless I'm with my partner, but I can't force that opinion on anyone else; couples are divided on this issue, and as long as both parties mutually agree to the terms of viewing pornography, there's no danger. Other couples say it's fine for their partners to visit strip clubs, either together or alone – and plenty of married couples bring third and fourth partners into the bedroom. Nobody worth your time is going to tell you where to draw the line in your own private life.

The issue of what's considered inappropriate outside the relationship is just another set of ground rules for a couple, and the only people who can set those are the ones who intend to follow and enforce them. Just don't let it turn into an issue of pride because then he *will* start doing it out of spite, and loudly.

As for the talk show situation, let's start with the wife. She makes a valid point; why is he ogling other women? Why is he being so noticeable about it? And more important, why doesn't she feel secure in this marriage? I think her leash is a bit too short, and this is why she's in the wrong.

Adults are not so different from children when it comes to breaking the rules. We still want thrills, and that includes the occasional peak at the green grass on the other side. You don't tell a child his Christmas presents are somewhere in the house and that he isn't allowed to look for them. If you do, you know he will look for them when you're gone. Even if he doesn't, you will always assume he did. However, if you never even bring up the topic of hiding his Christmas presents or even keeping them anywhere near the house, you won't really know if he tried to look. You won't even know if he thought about looking. And odds are, he probably won't look.

Similarly, you can't tell your partner he isn't allowed to look at other women if you never caught him doing it. Who knows whether he actively ogles women in public? But if you tell him, unprovoked, not to do it, you've planted a seed. You set a needless rule, and that's not fair to his ego.

The wife on the talk show wants a faithful man and a bit of re-assurance from time to time, but she's going about it the wrong way. Women, if you want your guy not to look at other girls, you have to approach it respectfully. Don't give him a reason to defy you. He's a man; he won't follow rules just because you set them. You want someone who will share or at least respect your ideals rather than submissively adhere to them.

Focusing back on the husband, he has just as much fault in this as she does. His wife did not necessarily approach him about this in a hostile and controlling manner, and there is no evidence that he has any right to be spiting her at every turn. While his wife needs to give him enough credit and trust him to be respectful to her, he needs to actually step up and show that respect.

If the couple had come to me for advice, I'd have to tell them how to compromise. While I believe most people are capable of handling it on their own, it's late in the game for this married couple. They need a formula to decide on a middle ground if the marriage is to succeed. That formula is something along the lines of *boys will be boys, but boys are not exempt from considering the feelings of others.* I'm not a marriage counselor, but I can at least take them back to once upon a time when this conversation should have taken place, when she first realized it made her uncomfortable to see her husband checking out other women. At this point, the most effective way to save the marriage is for him to stop doing it. I hope he did.

I'm always and forever asking women about how they would feel if their boyfriend did X, Y, or Z. In this situation, most women seem to understand that everyone steals a look from time to time, but the important thing is not acting on it and maybe not being so vocal about it. Many couples will even have casual conversations about who is attractive among their friends, or they'll make a game out of pointing out attractive people or mismatched couples at a public place. This, to me, is a fantastic way to deal with insecurity: Confront the situation head on, make it a couple's activity, and give each other the reassurance we all crave sometimes.

I urge every couple to sit down and have a conversation about infidelity – what it means to both of you, where the boundaries are, and what makes you uncomfortable. In the end, you might be surprised what you learn about each other's ideals. You can set some ground rules, and if you're respectful about it, he will respect you.

In front of you, at least.

## *'I Think He's Watching Us'*

COLLEGE CAMPUSES are pretty big, but damned if the dorm rooms aren't the size of small kitchens. On the other side of that kitchen could be a roommate who doesn't seem to ever go anywhere, save for the occasional trip to the public shower. Getting time to yourself is hard enough, but what if you have a significant other who also doesn't get much privacy? Now there's a problem.

For the millions of dorm and apartment-dwelling students in college, living alone is financially out of the question. A lot of students live in houses or condos with more than one roommate. It seems like people are in and out at all hours, and when you and your partner are in the mood, one thing's for sure: Someone else is home. That can be fine for the high fives that ensue after a one-night stand, but if you're in a serious relationship with someone, the sound or the sight of you having sex with your partner is probably not something you want to broadcast.

In a house or an apartment, you at least have the freedom to shut the door, but you're still faced with the fact that someone in the house is aware of what you're doing in there. It's just the thought that someone could be listening at the door, or that a roommate might think it's funny to install a webcam in your bedroom – and not to mention the noises that can carry through the air of a quiet night. It's enough to scare you away from getting intimate anywhere outside of a bomb shelter.

I know quite a few couples who are just very private people. They don't like to talk about their sex lives, and they definitely don't like to enact it within sight or earshot of a roommate they barely know. Sometimes, it's not even about modesty, but rather consideration. Couples understand that the last thing a dorm-mate wants to come home to is the sight of you and your partner having sex within five or six feet of his bed.

I met a couple my freshman year in college who had an extremely active sex life; they didn't mind talking about it, but they weren't going to put on a show for roommates or neighbors. They had been together since high school, where privacy was easy in the upstairs bedroom of his parents' house. But they were put in dorms the next year, much to the dismay of the couple and their respective libidos. This couple did not want to put sex on hold or even do it less frequently. So, into the van they went.

Unfortunately, this isn't an option for most people in a similar situation. Some college students don't even have cars on campus, let alone a vehicle big enough to accommodate any activity outside of saving the environment.

The obvious options for couples who don't have privacy are to seek out places that do offer privacy. That would include cheap hotels and mysterious abandoned buildings. One is costly and a bit sleazy (but effective), and the other is unrealistic and just a tad dangerous. If you're truly in a situation where you have no privacy, you just have to make do with what you got.

The dorm situation has been a problem among sexually active students for decades, but plenty of couples have been able to work out a system with their respective roommates. I don't agree with the idea of putting up a sign that tells a roommate to come back later or expecting him to leave every time you want to have sex, but couples can at least ask for a five-minute grace period when the roommate comes to the door, giving them time to get dressed. Besides, signals as obvious as the traditional rubber band or a less-than-subtle note are just going to breed curiosity and incite harassment from other people in the residence halls.

Couples can also alternate dorms, so the burden of compromising with the roommate doesn't always rest on his or her shoulders. Then again, some people have roommates who refuse to be dictated as to when they can enter their own dorm, and you can't blame them. Being restricted from their living space usually means they don't have access to their computer or maybe something they have to grab at the last minute, like a textbook. Therefore, another solution that has been proven effective is the privacy curtain. It costs money, but it prevents the roommate from seeing anything. If he comes home early, just quietly get dressed behind the curtain.

In situations where you have your own room, things are easier. First, there's the shower. Hop in the tub and turn on the water. No one will hear a thing. Even easier is keeping the door locked in the bedroom and turning on some upbeat music to drown out the noise. If you don't have a lock and you've got roommates who like to barge in on you, there's always the privacy curtain idea. But then again, if you have a roommate like that, it's best to forcefully and mercilessly nip that in the bud right away.

Still, there are couples who are so shy and private that these generic little ideas are out of the question, because it's the idea of someone being on the other side of the door – knowing what they're doing – that scares them to death. They can surrender to the fact that sexual encounters will be few and far between, but sometimes it's just *one* partner who's shy, while the other one couldn't care less who's watching.

It can physically and psychologically affect a relationship if the couple is hindered from fulfilling their basic needs. In this case, you have to be understanding of your partner's modesty; it's not something you can change easily. Instead, cherish the times where you can actually enjoy sex without the risk of being disturbed. In between those moments, spend a little more time observing the errand habits of your roommate. For example, how long does he usually spend at the grocery store? Maybe he has an early class. Keep time on his daily activities. Hell, make a chart – we can accomplish amazing things when it's a matter of sex or no sex.

And I guarantee that given enough time of no sex, your partner will start being more receptive to those five-minute quickies while the roommate is taking a shower.

## *Girlfriend-Kid Deluxe Combo*

CHILDREN ARE not just the future of this world's success, but also the future of our love lives, which, frankly, are more important to us than world issues sometimes. Kids change everything.

This one's mostly for the guys.

Meet a 21-year-old college student named "Brad." Brad lives in a dorm, and he met the woman of his dreams a month ago – a 24-year-old college graduate. They hit it off immediately and went on several dates. They learned so much about each other that they now feel like best friends. They've been physically intimate together, and it's been eight dates since they first met. He's ready to make it official, and so is she. But there's one last thing she has to get squared away. If Brad wants to be with her, he has to accept her daughter as well.

What the hell? She has a kid?

Brad really likes this woman. He's been single all through college, dating and waiting for the perfect match to come along, and here she is. But Brad was a bachelor with only his own decisions to worry about, and the woman he's now drawn to has a child. He knows there is a lot of baggage that comes with dating a single parent. Is Brad ready for this?

In an ideal situation, Brad would have known what he was getting into right away. On the first date, he would have found out about the child, and he would've been able to make a decision early on, before he fell for her.

But the majority of people I've talked to about this received the "I have a child" bombshell several dates later, after the attraction and connection had become solid. Most of the time they're angry, because they feel it was dishonest for their dates to hide something so major. In that case, they feel deceived and end the courtship immediately. After all, once a liar, always a liar, right?

It's different in this situation. Single parents know the stigma. There are countless generic little advice articles out there that stress how dangerous it is to date a single parent, especially a single mom. The savvy single mom realizes that most people believe all single moms are out to find a father figure. People think that they're all quick to latch on to any man who appears stable or wealthy, holding on with the grip of a gorilla. And then there's the idea that a single mom won't be able to invest in the relationship completely, because it will always be about the kid. It's also believed that you'll have to be the one who foots the bill for all of her child's expenses, or else you'll look unsupportive.

Single moms understand that all of these generalizations have truth in many cases, so when it comes to dating, they want the chance to prove themselves differently to a man before addressing the kid situation. It's technically dishonest, but it doesn't necessarily define a dishonest person.

Having fallen for the woman, Brad's decision is made with the consideration of his feelings for her, rather than the imprinted mindset that he should cherish his bachelor years as long as he can. If he can't handle it, it's because he can't handle the responsibilities of having a child, especially one who belongs to another man. It's not because he's been trained to instantly steer clear of women with kids, which might have been the case had he learned about the kid before getting to know her. Brad knows that being with her means being with the total package, and supporting her means supporting her daughter. The kid should not be taken lightly; children require more commitment than adults and can be just as affected by a breakup.

As a college student, your decision to date a single parent should be made based on your connection with that person, as well as your ability to handle a child. While you aren't necessarily going to be thrust into the parental role, you will be expected to become part of the child's life in due time, whether the child wants you to or not.

For Brad, he knew being a father figure would be a little easier if the kid never had a father around, but if the father is still in the picture, the child might view him as a contender to take the real father's role away.

But as the new boyfriend, Brad should understand it's the father's and mother's child either way – not his. It will always be that way.

Another issue you will have to face is financial responsibility. There aren't many college students who can afford to live on their own without parental help, let alone contribute to the well-being of their partner's offspring. But entering a long-term relationship with a single mom implies that you will eventually become more than the mother's new boyfriend – you'll become part of the family.

Or perhaps your girlfriend has been a single mother for a while and has the resources to support herself and her child. That would be a good scenario for someone like Brad, who could have grants, loans, and parental support that comprises just enough to feed and clothe him while he earns his degree.

Ideally, your new long-term partner should be able to wait a reasonable amount of time for you to get a self-supporting job before expecting the financial assistance she most likely needs. If you're fortunate enough to be in that situation, you can rest assured that you probably haven't gotten yourself into the replacement-dad trap, where you were finagled into a relationship and, inevitably, instant parenthood.

One final and major responsibility you have to consider is the concept of parenting in general. Odds are, your girlfriend has developed her own tried and true parenting techniques, and she wants to instill *her* lessons and *her* ideals into the child. Don't be a disciplinarian before that invitation has been extended.

When you get the news about her child, all of this can be sorted out with good communication. The only way to know what's expected of you in this situation is to ask. The good news is that communication will be easy. A single mother likely has the experience to know what she needs from a relationship. A single mother doesn't have time to be coy or wait for a man to make his move or make wild guesses. She probably won't hesitate to tell you her needs and exactly what she expects from you. If you can handle it, I don't see why you shouldn't.

# 4

# The Hard Part

College relationships don't necessarily have to end just because it's "not fun" at the moment, though it might be tempting to stay in the mindset that experimenting and having fun is in your nature. Sometimes, you just hit rough spots that require a little guidance and patience. Other times, you just come to a point where it has to end.

This chapter briefly addresses the common relationship-ending events of college love. The known hardships of long-distance love can make you want to give up before even trying, and the psychological damage of an abusive partner can make you wonder if love is worth trying again. The death of romance can push you away before attempting to revive it, and the pain of infidelity often drives us to do irrational things. Whatever the trouble may be, it's sometimes impossible to mentally and emotionally prepare for the damage it can cause.

If you're engulfed in the hard part of your relationship, read this chapter before you decide what to do next.

## *Sexy Saturday*

WHETHER YOU wait until marriage or do it immediately, there might come a time in your relationship where sex just loses its novelty. This might sound like something that's normally addressed many years into a marriage, but I see it happening more and more often with long-term college couples who have been together for just a few years.

When you get past the "bunny" stage of the relationship, the decision to have sex becomes more judicious, and you eventually get to the point where there's too much else to do – and sex takes too much time. At first, you couldn't keep your hands off your partner, and now you'd rather sleep in another room so you can get a full night's sleep. Couples who get into this slump tend to make up for it by making a point to schedule sex, and some shorten it by skipping foreplay.

A friend of mine named "Jessica" consulted me about spicing things up with her long-term boyfriend, who had become just as bored with intercourse as she was. Jessica said it was different when he still enjoyed it. While sex was never as important to her, Jessica understood that her boyfriend really liked it, and she knew that it was important to maintain an active sex life, especially at such a young age. Jessica and her boyfriend were only 23 years old at the time, so it came as a shock to them when it got to the point where neither partner was excited about having sex anymore.

They tried to set aside one day a week where they would get intimate in the evening, no matter what. They even gave it a cutesy name: "Sexy Saturday." But Sexy Saturday was a short-lived endeavor. When Saturday evening arrived, there was usually something else to do – go out with friends, give the dog a bath, or watch a movie rental that's due back the next day. There just didn't seem to be any excitement about copulating. They had done it so many times, so why make a point to do it regularly when masturbation is actually more convenient?

Some of you are probably in awe that anyone at that age could be bored with sex already, but it's more common than couples care to admit. After doing the same thing a few hundred times, sex could become a chore, a necessary task to occasionally relieve stress. It becomes something you start to do only when there's nothing on TV, or when you're drunk.

Getting bored with it mostly stems from predictability – over the years you've learned what your partner likes and doesn't like, and you have it down to a science; everything has always played out the same, from the initial kiss to the afterglow. It's about as exciting as a car wash.

Couples like Jessica and her boyfriend will admit that they have not done much experimentation in the bedroom. For them, sexual enjoyment has mostly been the result of one or two Q&A sessions, where they tell each other what feels good. But our tastes change, and we adapt by nature. The same sexual routine not only gets boring, but it also starts to feel all wrong. Jessica said it has been a long time since she and her boyfriend asked each other what they liked.

Some say a physical connection is only a small part of the bond between two lovers, and they argue that when the sexual spark dies down, it doesn't mean the bond between them fades. But I think it can, and it does. In Jessica's relationship, as sex started to become a mundane chore, the frequency of conflict and fights began to escalate. Without the joy of sex to remind them that getting physically intimate is a small but very important part of being in love, they used other things to fill the void. It's not uncommon to resort to blowing petty differences out of proportion due to that subconscious feeling that something is missing. Often someone perceives this missing spark as a sign the relationship is not meant to continue any longer. The fights are open doors.

Why end a relationship because of one bump in the road? That bump can be smoothed over with the cement of love. And the jackhammer of understanding, as well as the construction worker of communication.

Additional metaphors go here: _____.

Sex or some form of physical intimacy is usually not optional in long-term relationships, especially so early in the game. It's definitely not something you can start and then allow to fade away over time. It was once a major part of your relationship, and if you let it go, it will be missed. And it can be missed long before marriage. Don't assume the excitement of the honeymoon will revive your otherwise dull sex life. It could do just the opposite, when you wind up doing it the same way in the same positions as you've always done. Oh no, it's the sudden realization that you'll be having the same sex for the rest of your life.

Address the issue now, and keep addressing it. No topic should be taboo for people in love, though it sometimes can be hard to talk about sexual issues in fear that it might be a one-sided conversation. The key to a successful sex life – and, ultimately, a successful relationship – is to accept that if one person isn't satisfied, no one is satisfied. That even applies to Jessica, who claims she doesn't always need sex to be happy. Even so, Jessica needs to at least enjoy it when she does need it.

There are plenty of ways to spice up your sex life, the simplest one being to plan a date night and court each other like you did when you first met. Some couples take a nice vacation in seclusion, away from life's obligations – provided time and finances permit.

If that's not for you, however, there is always the sex toy route. I find that many couples who have quickly grown bored of sex never had the nerve to buy a sex toy or even bring up the topic of having one. There's also the misconception that sex toys are meant only as replacements for actual sex – a masturbation aid, if you will. Not so. Check the Internet for a few fun ideas.

You can search online or in sex-advice books to find something fun and unique that suits you. It's not important what you do to revive or maintain your sex life, but it is important that you do it as a couple. The first step is acknowledging that your sex life isn't all of what you want. The second step is being willing to address it, making more of an effort than penciling in another Sexy Saturday.

## Doing It Over The Phone

SAMANTHA twirls the phone cord around her pinky and giggles.

"What are you wearing right now?" she asks, using the sexiest voice she can muster at three in the morning.

"A turtleneck," her boyfriend, Jared, replies.

Silence on the other end of the line.

"It's really cold in New York," he adds.

"Oh."

Poor Samantha. After an easy two years of being a college couple, her boyfriend graduated and got a job. And that job requires he spend the next ten months in New York, nine hundred miles away from home. Samantha couldn't tag along because she has another year left of school. They want to make it work and even hope to get married one day. Is it possible?

According to just about every related study, it probably won't work. The distance from each other usually turns into emotional disconnection, trust issues quickly arise, and both people decide it's just not worth it. Often, people end up being unfaithful to their partners in a vulnerable moment of loneliness. Couples know this, and they probably know someone who went through the same thing, so trust becomes an obstacle within the first couple of months.

Couples can also grow apart when they get the opportunity to try new things. Samantha's boyfriend could decide he likes living in New York and plans to seek permanent employment there, while she wants to stay close to family. Samantha might even later learn that her boyfriend met someone in New York, which is the real reason he wants to stay.

A long-distance relationship is the ultimate test of love; there are just so many things that can happen during that time apart, and most of them lead to a breakup. But should that stop you from trying? Certainly not. It's mostly true that long-distance love doesn't last, but I encourage you to make every effort to be the exception to that rule.

Remaining close even in distance is the key, and there are plenty of ways to do that. However, the first thing you need is motivation. If you're not serious about a long-term relationship with your partner, it's pointless to make an effort to maintain anything long distance if you've already planned to end it regardless. If you're still in that "let's wait and see" stage, I can almost guarantee your long-distance relationship will fail. In that state of mind, there's nothing tying you together as a couple, and a bird in hand…well, you know the saying. Both of you have to want it. A lot. Can you imagine yourself with someone else? If you can, you will probably end up with someone else.

An important part of staying close is communication. Do it every day, whether it's a phone call, an instant message conversation, or an e-mail exchange. Plenty of couples who live in the same town still talk on the phone or online every day. If you're a thousand miles apart, you have no excuse. And even e-mail is questionable as real communication – and text messaging certainly doesn't count – but it's sometimes all that's possible if your schedules conflict.

I still recommend taking several days out of the week for real conversations, and maybe even getting webcams for pseudo-face-to-face interaction. The sound of your partner's voice or even the sight of each other's smiles can go a long way in confirming an emotional presence.

You should go even further than a phone call or an instant message to show each other how much you care, or else things could still go flat. The communication can get bland and routine, and your partner might suspect that you're only doing it to keep up the façade that you are being completely faithful.

I know of a couple who still went on dates together even when they were hundreds of miles apart. They would have dinner "together" by ordering or cooking the same kind of food, setting up a video conference on the computer, and talking on the phone. The couple would occasionally have a movie night, where they would go to their respective video stores, rent the same movie, and watch it at the same time while talking about it on the phone.

Some couples send each other care packages with their partner's favorite candy, perfume, flowers, cologne, love letters, and sexy photos and videos. I recommend sending the packages to each other at the same time and opening them together while on the phone. Doing these things as a couple, even in distance, will contribute to preserving another important issue: trust.

When you're away from each other, it will be easy to cheat; it will be convenient to cheat. And after six months of physical intimacy with righty and lefty, it will probably be extremely tempting to cheat. You can't assume the worst, or else the worst will happen. What you should realize, however, is that cheating is cheating regardless of location. If your partner cheats on you, there's nothing you can do about it except understand that you're dating a cheater and take the proper action. Again, long distance will test the strength of your relationship. If something like that happens, you now know how strong it really is. Do with that information what you will.

You should also accept that your partner could cheat on you and you may never find out. But that applies to more than just long-distance relationships. People who live together can still get away with lying and cheating; obviously, you can't spend your life wondering about your partner's every move. Trust.

Throughout all the communication and shared moments, you should also be saving up and waiting for the opportunity to visit your partner. To make it quicker and easier, both of you should save up for one plane ticket, but one of you will actually do the flying. And while this will be the ultimate opportunity to make up for several sexless months, you should also use the trip to calmly, rationally address any issues that concern or worry you. In the event of an argument, you want to be there to smooth things over. It's much better than resolving conflict over the phone, where someone has the opportunity to hang up and hastily do something regrettable.

Long-distance relationships *can* work, but it will be an uphill battle that requires effort from both of you. If one of you fails in that effort, don't feel any worse than you would feel after a normal breakup. The odds were against you.

## *An Epic Adventure*

ENJOY YOUR first apartment. It's probably tiny with outdated appliances. But if you're financially fortunate enough for something better than that, count yourself lucky that you'll have more space between each other when you need it. And you will need it.

People say there are oodles of reasons why couples shouldn't live together before getting married, but most of them can't stand on their own two feet without the crutch of religion. However, some traditionalists do frown upon living together before marriage because it increases the pressure to stay in the relationship even if you shouldn't, and the couple eventually gets a divorce when it becomes too difficult to tolerate each other, though they should not have gotten married in the first place.

That pressure, I presume, comes from co-ownership. Couples who live together might end up getting a pet, merging bank accounts, buying furniture together, and having more mutual friends. Some unmarried couples even get a mortgage together. Once everything is so fused together financially, the convenience of staying a couple often masks deeper problems that would have otherwise been addressed earlier in the relationship.

That's a good point, and I agree with it. There are plenty of valid reasons not to move in together before marriage, and you can count on me to be the first to discourage such a thing with certain couples. But my aim is not give you good reasons to reconsider moving in together, but to make sure you're moving in together for good reasons.

There are encyclopedias of information about living with your partner, ones that provide legal tips and others that give you spiritual guidance or something ridiculous like that. I encourage you to consult those resources if you're having doubts, because moving in together is a big step; couples can benefit from as much research and advice as possible. I, on the other hand, only wish to provide you with the basics – the common problems you will face and how to solve them. My philosophy is that if you're ready to move in, these concepts will be all you really need to make it work. Don't act too surprised.

Unlike sex, successful cohabitation with your partner requires love. It requires patience and compromise, and it definitely requires tolerance to an extreme. Some people move in together unprepared to change their lifestyles.

It can be a shocking switch, or it can be smooth; you'll know which one it will be when you're ready to do it. And while I advocate premarital cohabitation, I only advise it for couples who plan on getting married or making some other form of long-term commitment. In fact, it's best for engaged couples to move in together, not just couples who could see themselves together in the long run. If you live together just for the sake of convenience without making any solid long-term plans to stay together (whether you believe in marriage or not), you could wind up falling into that comfort trap, where it's harder to break up even when it's necessary.

Compromising living environments will be difficult, especially when you find out she wants to bring her furniture along, and there is simply no room for that huge bed you've been attached to for nearly a decade. You might like your band posters and shot glass collection, but it clashes with her grand plan of decorating with a theme. But the biggest stab in the heart will be when you find out she doesn't think all your liquor should be displayed on the kitchen counter.

And then there's that gigantic picture of her grandmother that she wants to display in the living room. However, you think your "Duel of the Siths" *Star Wars* poster would look better.

But you know better, and so does she. It has to be a neutral household with neutral decorations, a compromise split down the middle. But it's not about putting up just as much guy stuff as girl stuff – it's selecting the décor that looks classier and buying the rest together. Select neutral styles and neutral colors. But keep note of who buys any household items; in the event of a breakup, those items will belong to that person.

Guys often make the mistake of assuming that "pretty" means "girly," but this is not the case. Hang on to your testicles, but a beautiful painting of magnolias, for example, is not a compromise in favor of the woman. It's neutral and does not suggest a feminine household. A fuzzy pink rug in the living room, though, is not a compromise.

She might not like the concept of displaying a bunch of shot glasses, but if the shot glasses are unique and classy, they can effectively occupy a corner shelf – but in return, you should let her display something feminine that isn't over-the-top gaudy. By the way, a shot glass that says "Caution: Instant sex machine. Just add alcohol" is *not* classy.

Of course, decorating your house is dependent on your tastes as a couple, and the examples I described above are as random as they come. Even when a couple has similar decorating tastes, location becomes a problem. I knew an artsy couple who filled their apartment walls with their own paintings; the conflict was not on how to decorate, but on whose art got the most prominent viewing for guests.

She wanted her biggest painting on the front living room wall, and so did he. It was a simple compromise, however: They each hung a smaller painting side by side instead. The larger ones went in the bedroom. I think it's a good compromise for any couple if there's an issue of location; the sentimental but disagreeable stuff should go in the bedroom.

When it comes to decorating together, compromising is not an option. Even if you don't care how it looks and you want your partner to make all the decisions, you have to force yourself to provide at least some input. Otherwise, you wind up in a situation where your partner was able to take control, and often this will make it more difficult for you request changes in the future. Believe me.

Decorating is only a small part of the compromise in organization. At your partner's old place, whether it was another apartment or his parents' house, you might have noticed a certain level of cleanliness. The place could be immaculate, but never assume it's your partner's doing. Check out the bedroom on an off-day, and that will give you an idea of what your mate will deem an acceptable everyday neatness level at the new apartment.

Women are generally cleaner and neater than men, but it can sometimes be the exact opposite. I've seen one too many advice columns where women complain that their boyfriend or husband is a neat freak. I often wonder how much of a neat freak the guy really is. Does he have OCD, or does she refuse to pick up her dirty macaroni and cheese bowls off the floor?

Immediately deciding on an acceptable level of cleanliness is important. Some people don't feel that their living space needs to be immaculate, while others care deeply about maintaining order and keeping stress levels down in the environment. But it can really be stressful if the couple doesn't share the same ideals about staying neat.

If you're strongly in opposition, the easiest way to solve this problem is to meet halfway. If he's messy and you're obsessed with a clean house, set aside one day every two weeks where both of you do a thorough cleaning with an equal share of housework.

Divide the chores accordingly, or do it together. But the important thing is to do it at the same time on the same day. It will get done, and it won't be a daily battle between his reprehensible sloppiness and your psychotic need to be sterile. The everyday chores can be divided and compromised.

But even cleanliness issues can't hold a candle to the conflict caused by the most important part of living together: money. Hardly anyone ever fully agrees on how to spend money, and this can make or break a long-term relationship. All I can say about that is keep things separate until marriage. All of it. Save for the responsibility of rent and utilities, nothing in that place should belong to both of you. Bills should be split down the middle – none of that "I pay the electricity, you pay cable" nonsense. Everything is equal, regardless of how often someone is home or whether you use less electricity than your partner. If someone can't afford half the bills, you should not be living together. If your partner is jobless and doesn't plan to work when you get married, then don't live together until then.

Finally, remember to maintain a healthy amount of time together and time apart. Moving in together doesn't necessarily mean you no longer have to plan around each other's schedules for romance. You'll still have separate lives and responsibilities to fulfill, and just because you come home to each other doesn't mean you're spending more time together. Exclusive date nights remind you why you're in love with the person – couples often believe a romance has inevitably died without making the effort to keep it alive.

But don't get me wrong; separate alone time is just as important. You're in love, so you should be comfortable with giving each other space, even if it's just physical space between each other in the room. Being in tune with your partner and knowing when to give comfort and when to just be quiet for a while can prevent a lot of fights.

You might find the preceding advice to be too basic and too generic because it lays everything out like there's only one way to do it, and it simplifies the process to seem easier than it actually is. You might tell me that couples have many more problems than decorating and money and that moving in together is never so simple. That's correct; it probably won't be as easy for you as I described. Compromise is hard.

Therefore, if you haven't reached the stage in your relationship where compromise is second nature, don't move in together yet.

## *When It Gets Old*

IT HAS been said a thousand times that the first five years of marriage are the most difficult, but I've learned it can get difficult in the first five years of any romantic relationship, married or not. There comes a certain point when the "fun" is over, your love has been declared, and the living begins. Ultimately, this is when you start finding out whether it's a love that will stick.

It gets difficult to sustain the relationship after so long because there's not much else to learn about each other. There is no more mystery, and even the romance has kind of leveled off. If you're living together, you've essentially fused lives. If you're still in school, you're both working your asses off to pay the bills. You have come to a point where you are still hanging out together, still having sex, and still going to social functions together – but you've forgotten why. You reach a certain point where you question the bond: It's been five years. You no longer get butterflies in your stomach when your partner walks into the room. You no longer blush when you hold hands. Even that tingly fireworks feeling is gone when you kiss. Have you fallen out of love?

It's possible, but probably not. Couples start fighting a lot during this stage of their relationship because it feels like there's nothing else left to do. The minuscule disagreements are the only thing you feel like you can share, so you blow them up bigger than they should ever be. The fights become so frequent that you may just decide *if this is what it's going to be like with him on a daily basis, I want out right now.*

Sometimes, after a person begins to think there's nothing more to learn from her partner, she gets scared. She believes it means they are growing apart. Perhaps it wasn't meant to be, or else it just wasn't meant to go any further than now.

What she doesn't understand, however – because of all the romance she sees on TV and all the budding relationships around her – is that every couple goes through the same stage. It's the threshold of infatuation. You have become your complete, true self around your partner, and so has he around you. You no longer feel the need to put on a show to impress each other, but this does *not* mean you are growing apart.

It means you are reaching a stage in life where you can make a real, educated decision about whether the relationship is really worth continuing. A worthy relationship is not about the emotional high of New Relationship Syndrome or the euphoria from the best orgasm of your life. And it's certainly not about how often you cuddle on the couch vs. how often you just sit together and watch TV. Those aspects can contribute to a happy relationship, but it mostly boils down to whether you are still in love with each other. So, how do you know if the love is still there? I can give you some rough guidelines.

Mainly, what do you think? Has there been a nagging issue

with your partner that you've never been able to get through? Does your intuition tell you to end it? And by intuition, I don't mean your perception of the relationship in this very moment. I mean as a whole – are you happy?

Before you answer that, ask yourself what it means to be happy. If you think there is such a scenario where you will live in ecstasy with your partner every day, you should reevaluate your idea of romantic happiness.

Being happy with your partner means that no matter what conflict arises, you are always able to solve it completely and justly. No matter what temptations have come along, you were always able to bypass them; whether it was difficult or not, you ultimately realized you were better off in your current relationship.

Happiness with your partner is also defined by your willingness to be together. Do you look forward to your partner coming home each day, or do you always get that sinking feeling that your conflict-free afternoon is over? Ask yourself how often you would choose a night out with your friends over an intimate night in the bedroom with your partner.

When conflict and fights do occur, think about how willing you are to resolve them. Is it easier to walk away from them and come back when both of you have cooled off, or do you still sit together and have it out until you've reached a resolution?

And how much does your partner's opinion matter to you? Do you still ask each other for advice or insight in most situations, or do you no longer value or respect what he has to say?

People ask me whether it's time to end their relationship based on a recent fight or even a series of recent fights. They often see these frequent conflicts as a sign of the end, because the romance is gone and the "reality" is starting to come through. When I ask people those easy questions about love and happiness, *most of the time* they realize how much their partner still means to them. They still want to get intimate more often than not, they still look forward to seeing each other, and even when those fights can get quite ugly, they face it full force and never just wait for the issue to go away. And most of all, they still rely heavily on each other's opinions.

But I said *most of the time.*

Sometimes, we just get to a point in our relationships where re-evaluation is necessary, and it doesn't always produce positive results. It may not be your fault, but if you no longer have respect for your partner, please allow him to find someone who does.

## *No Excuse For Abuse*

"YOU NEED to talk about abusive relationships in your book," a friend told me.

The topic didn't cross my mind as I interviewed couples in preparation for this book. Most of my ideas come from issues I have addressed personally, and no one has ever said, "Dear Stephen, I'm being abused. Please help."

Victims of abuse might get out of the relationship immediately, while others feel trapped or that they owe it to their partners to try and make it work – or else they don't realize the abuse is a problem at all. In any case, you don't see many college students crying out for help against what I can only imagine is a terrible situation.

Obviously, you should have no reason to ever fear your significant other. If you feel like you are being intimidated, threatened, physically hurt, emotionally drained, or otherwise insecure over the future of your well-being, you are probably in an abusive relationship. There is no excuse for abuse.

For a good source of information about the types of abuse and what you can do about it, visit www.letswrap.com. It's a small organization based out of southwest Michigan, but a quick Internet search made me believe it's one of the most comprehensive guides for abuse that doesn't involve legal fees or purchasing other books.

Most of the information you need will be on the site, but I will share with you now one tidbit of guidance I feel is especially important – if not obvious – for those who feel abuse can be justified.

Taken directly from the site, here are a few myths (i.e. falsities) about domestic abuse:

1. "Good wives" and "nice girls" don't get battered.
2. Batterers abuse their partners because they love them.
3. Domestic abuse is confined to the poor, disadvantaged, uneducated, particular age or ethnic groups.
4. Battered women provoke their own abuse and battering.
5. Battered women like to be abused or battered.
6. Alcohol and drugs cause battering.
7. All a battered woman has to do is call the police and deal with the situation.

I'd like to add one more point to that: Just because you're young does not mean you have time to work out abuse problems without help.

## *Hey, Snoopy!*

IN MY earlier years of "professional" writing, I was a technology columnist. I gave computer advice. I wrote about buying home theatre systems and setting up TV tuners in PCs. And one day, I got this letter:

*Dear Stephen,*

*I was wondering if you knew of any good hacking programs or methods of getting someone's e-mail password. I suspect my girlfriend of cheating, and I want to be sure.*

*-Anonymous*

At this point in my budding career, I was still trying to find my niche in writing, and given my background in working with computers, I thought technology would be my best bet. While I offered advice to young couples via other means, I never thought of actually having an advice column, nor had I ever been presented with the opportunity. I had a good idea of what to say about this reader's situation, but my reply was for comedic value, exploiting the irony of the "Tech Guy" giving relationship advice. I present to you the column that started it all:

Dear Anonymous,

Yes, I do. However, it's illegal, so you're on your own there.

On a different note, let's take a step back and look at this situation. You say you suspect your girlfriend is cheating on you. Do you suspect she's having some sort of online relationship, or do you think she's communicating with someone via e-mail because it's more secure? Hacking into her e-mail account may give you the answers you're looking for, but ask yourself this: What answers are you looking for?

Something tells me you may already be in the mindset that the relationship is over. You are intending to do something indisputably dishonest, while your girlfriend may or may not be doing something dishonest.

There's something wrong with the relationship; that's obvious.

Two wrongs do not make a right. If you want to preserve what bond you and your girlfriend still have, the best way to approach this situation is with the cliché "talk to her" method. Don't accuse her, and don't raise your voice. Tell her about your insecurities. Tell her how you feel. Tell her about the changes you've noticed. Women want honesty in a relationship; who doesn't?

You'll be able to find out more from her if you communicate with her, keeping an open mind. Most importantly, the conversation shouldn't be all about her problems, either. Admit that you have some issues to work out, and ask her about the changes she may be seeing in you.

Finding out someone is cheating on you is a hard pill to swallow. Reading her e-mail is an irrational action that will likely lead to other irrational actions, ultimately destroying a relationship that can be repaired.

Not exactly prize-winning writing – or even insightful advice for that matter. It's too generic and horribly cliché for my taste, and I don't think anyone can benefit from being told that two wrongs don't make a right.

But I shared this column with you for two reasons: (1) It makes a good point that those who snoop are being blatantly dishonest without full knowledge that their partner is dishonest, and (2) It suggests that talking to your partner appropriately could reveal something without having to snoop. So, allow me to expand upon these points.

Snooping on your partner violates his trust, just as cheating would violate yours. But how else are you going to find out the truth? Do you think he'll ever admit it, or perhaps you'll come home one day to find the evidence dangling in front of your face? Clichés like lipstick on his collar, the panties in the back seat of the car, and the misplaced love letter are all possible, but not likely. You can't expect a cheater to necessarily be dumb; they don't all get caught, sadly.

Still, you don't have to see the obvious signs to suspect your partner is cheating. Undisclosed phone calls, late-night trips to the office, and the smell of another woman's perfume are all convenient little telltale signs, but sometimes a cheater doesn't need to cheat at night, and sometimes a cheater uses e-mail rather than the phone. So, if there aren't any surface signs, we can look at other changes in the relationship such as emotional distancing. Cheaters have also been known to become paranoid about their partners cheating on them; after all, he's getting away with it, so maybe you are, too.

I won't go over all the signs of a cheating partner, because you can get that information anywhere. Besides, much like a list of symptoms enables a hypochondriac, a list of cheater habits will get the paranoid partners into gear.

So let's assume you are in a situation where you absolutely know that your partner is cheating on you. You know because your intuition has been sounding the alarm for weeks, maybe even months – but the problem is, you don't have any physical evidence. You can't present a pair of rogue panties or a semen-stained pair of pants.

So, you want to prove it. And you are at liberty to do that, as long as you don't do anything that would put you in legal jeopardy. That means hacking into someone's personal e-mail might not be an option. But perhaps if he was dumb enough to give you his password without changing it, you could give that a go.

If you've got the money, you could hire a private investigator. If you've got the time, you can do your own public spying. You can scroll through his previously dialed numbers in his cell phone. You can ask your friends to spy on him in shifts. If you're feeling techie, you can put a key-logger on his computer that would record every keystroke he makes. Wow, there are so many ways to gather some hard evidence and present it to your partner. And then what? Is it time to break up?

If the answer is definitely yes, try skipping all of that, and end the relationship now. You're needlessly spending time with a cheater who you plan to dump anyway. You aren't married yet, and there is no law that says you must have evidence of infidelity before breaking up with someone. I suggest you end it on the grounds that the two of you are "growing apart" and save yourself the hassle of the confrontation and the denial – unless, of course, you need self-validation by embarrassing him.

If you need to be sure he's cheating before ending it, then you don't have enough reason to snoop in the first place. Snooping is the end of the relationship, so you don't want to be in a position where you look bad if you're wrong.

Of course, it's not always that simple, and I can't assume that everyone has an auto-breakup policy with cheaters. If that's the case, spying and snooping are not viable options; they'll just create more conflict. Maybe he cheated on you, but if you found out by snooping, you now have trust issues to address on both sides instead of just one side.

On that note, we can address the second valid point from that "tech support" column: communication.

What do you think will happen if you confront your partner and tell him you think he's cheating on you? Probably nothing good will come of it. He might admit it if he's looking for an out, but he'll probably just deny it and call you paranoid. He might even turn it into an argument about you and your "trust issues." Sometimes, in the heat of an argument, a cheater might confess for the sake of proving a point, but we can't count on that.

What a confrontation will do, however, is make him change his behavior. If he's really cheating, he now knows that you suspect it and will probably be more cautious or even over-compensate for his recent behavior. I've heard stories about cheaters buying their partners more gifts and being more affectionate than ever. In many cases, once he believes he has convinced you that he's faithful, that's when he gets sloppy and starts letting the physical evidence slip through.

It's important that the confrontation be as passive as possible. No ultimatums (e.g. "If you're cheating on me, it's over"). Don't accuse or insinuate anything. Instead, talk about where the relationship is falling short of ideal. If you believe he's cheating, you probably have noticed several of the many signs of infidelity – so address those without suggesting guilt. Tell him you want to work on preserving the relationship. Odds are, a cheater will deny that there are any problems, while a faithful person would be willing to consider your observations.

And remember, cheater or not, don't make the conversation all about his problems. Many people mistakenly believe they are the sole victim if their partner cheats, but if it has happened to you more than once, you may have an issue with the type of partners you select or your role in relationships. Just try to keep an open mind without branding yourself as the unlucky victim.

As you can see, you have several options when it comes to dealing with the suspicion of cheating. Notice that they all seem to have less-than-desirable outcomes for you. But you're probably being cheated on, so you have to do something about it, regardless of how it all plays out. Choose the one that's worth the possible consequences.

## *Cheated*

YOU SAY he's cheating on you. You caught him, someone else caught him, or he confessed – in any case, you have proof. You've decided to maintain a little dignity and end it now. But wait; he just dropped down to his knees and begged you for forgiveness. He swears it will never happen again. Now what?

LEAVE HIM.

But you love him! It was one mistake. Aren't we all human?

ONCE A CHEATER, ALWAYS A CHEATER.

That's not always true, damnit.

OK, fair enough.

Allow me to introduce you to "Katie," a recent college graduate looking to settle down and start a family and a new career. Her boyfriend of three years, "Brandon," is supposed to be that guy who starts a family with Katie. Brandon has graduated, too, and he has a nice job already. They are engaged, and he plans to buy a house in the next six months.

One night, Brandon decides to celebrate his recent success by going out with his closest buddies. He's got a good life ahead of him, and that's worth a drink or two. Or seven or eight. Suddenly, Brandon isn't a career man in a committed relationship; he's just a drunk, confused guy who's dancing with a cute blonde at a bar, and he doesn't know who she is or why they are grinding up against each other.

The rest of the night is a blur, and the next morning, when he wakes up next to that cute blonde from the bar, he knows he made a mistake.

Brandon confesses immediately; he cries and pleads, and Katie just sits there. She fights back the tears, though she has mixed emotions overall – he cheated, but he confessed; he still cheated, but he was not in his right state of mind. The ball is in her court.

People come to me with some variation of this story from time to time, and my response is almost always the same: If you take him back, start over. Start over with everything – that includes your trust, as well as the intensity of the relationship. If you're engaged, the wedding is postponed indefinitely.

If you live together, I recommend moving out, though I realize that's not always possible. Instead, become roommates and nothing more. Keep your distance for a while. He's no longer the long-term close boyfriend he once was, because he now has to show you he's capable of starting fresh and never making the same mistake again.

Having said that, make sure you *allow* him to work on regaining your trust. I cannot stress that enough. People often believe they have a right to hold something as bad as cheating over their significant others' heads. After all, he screwed up, not you. But if you do this, you are being counterproductive to making the relationship work. The decision to take him back was yours alone, and forgiveness comes with the territory. Do not harp on his infidelity; don't keep him in relationship limbo, where he can't leave but he can't go any further, either.

In Katie's situation, there are several things she and Brandon can work on together. The main thing: trusting him with his friends. Where were they, and what role did they play in this? The problem seems to be that everyone was equally drunk, so no one was able to keep the group tame. Can he be trusted to have a safe, faithful night out with his friends? Not right now. Besides, Brandon won't have time for friends; he has too much work to do to bring his relationship with Katie back to where it was. End of argument.

That was a lovely story about cheating, which describes the best-case scenario for someone whose trust has been betrayed. It's probably not that clear-cut for you.

So, imagine Brandon's decision to sleep with the blonde at the bar was a conscious one; he wasn't drunk, and he still decided to cheat. Would you still take him back if he confessed the next day? I believe this is still a gray area. Humans can have weak moments, and given that Brandon was engaged, he could be getting cold feet about spending the rest of his life with one person. It's still a sad excuse for cheating, but if you believe in second chances, you can start over in this case, too. It will be just as difficult. Your decision, not mine.

And now, imagine the most likely scenario: Katie finds out about it days, weeks or months later. Whether it's through Brandon's confession or evidence presented later, I hope you know what the practical decision is.

I've heard every excuse in the book from people who want to make things work with their cheating, lying partner. They say he had a vulnerable moment and was scared of admitting it and ruining the relationship; or perhaps he's sorry for lying and sincerely wants to start over.

I say let him start over with someone else.

The chances of a couple being able to completely move past such a serious infidelity are slim. There is more success in maintaining dignity and moving on than there is in trying to make a busted relationship function. The best relationship advicists will never condone staying with a liar and a cheater, and neither should you. I promise it will be more work than it's worth.

Just for fun, let's add another twist: Katie is carrying Brandon's baby. I've witnessed these circumstances before, and while it's not a pretty situation, the decision should be the same. Brandon might want forgiveness, but he's asking it of Katie, not of his unborn child. Katie does not have to be in a relationship with Brandon to motivate him to maintain his paternal duties. Whether or not Brandon takes care of his kid is a result of his character; if Brandon ever had any intention of being a trustworthy man, he would stay around to take care of his child. People who "get married for the baby" are placing too much value on the ideal definition of a family; they are cheating themselves – and the baby – out of happiness through realistic functionality.

There is life after infidelity – for both the cheater and the cheatee. But that life does not have to be together. Giving each other the freedom to start over in new relationships with new partners is the practical, healthy way to deal with infidelity.

But while it's difficult to fully trust someone who has wronged you, it's not impossible – if you wind up together again one day, just do yourself a favor and check his references. If you don't think you can ever fully forgive him, don't even try. You've been warned.

# 5

# **Aftermath**

It's the end. You've tried to work things out, but there's no point in fooling yourself anymore. Your significant other has shown you in more ways than one that there is no salvaging this relationship. So, what now?

There's a first time for everything, and many college students have asked me about the "aftermath" – meaning, how does one make a clean break, or what do you do if the ex tries to seek revenge?

This short and not-so-sweet chapter covers a few of the basics about the aftermath of a relationship, including the break-up process, the facts about rebounds, and damage control in the event of revenge. The chapter concludes with one final, important point: You do not have to be in a relationship to be happy.

## *Ending It*

THERE IS seldom a painless way to break up with someone, especially if you're ending a long-term relationship. Harsh words are exchanged, you openly or secretly blame each other, and you finally come to a fake resolution and try to remain "friends," or maybe you never speak to each other again.

Or scenario two: You break up and your ex continues to stalk you, make outrageous threats, and ultimately reaffirm your decision to end the relationship. Or three: It's a mutual breakup, everyone is happy, and you join arms and skip off into the sunset.

Whatever the case may be in the end, people are ever-searching for the best way to make a breakup as clean as possible. Unfortunately, that desire for an easy solution translates to a fear of confrontation. I cringe when someone tells me they left a "Dear John" or sent an e-mail. Even a phone call is less than ideal. A non-confrontational breakup will brand you a coward, no matter how eloquently written your letter is or how verbally adept you are on the phone. Let's call that rule number one for a respectful breakup: Do it in person.

Here's a fun question someone has asked me before: "Whenever we see each other, we always kiss first; how do I handle this if I plan to break up with him right after?"

To kiss or not to kiss. I say kiss. Odds are, your feelings for your partner didn't change overnight. The decision to break up is something you thought about long and hard, making sure you are doing the right thing. If you kissed him last time, kiss him this time. By not kissing him and then immediately sitting him down to talk, you've already broken up with him before you could even explain yourself. If you're looking for a clean breakup with the potential for friendship, you'd better be a fast talker at this point, as he's already upset. Go ahead with the kiss, but allow nothing more than that. You'll be forgiven for stealing a peck, but pre-breakup sex is just wrong.

The second rule is about location. Choose wisely. Some say doing it in a public place will prevent your partner from overreacting. If you want a clean get-out-of-my-life breakup, a public place might be OK, but for those who still want that glimmer of hope for friendship, I recommend being sensitive to your partner's feelings by doing it in private. The public breakup is another old non-confrontational trick, and it's just a step above doing it over the phone. Besides, who says he won't make a scene?

The third rule: Say the right things. Honesty is terrific, but politeness is usually better. Don't say anything that could possibly affect the way your partner sees himself. That's for him to figure out alone. The clichés like "It's not you, it's me" are popular for a reason. Your partner might beg for honesty, but you should spare his feelings for now. Developing a friendship after the breakup is going to take some time, and telling him something like he's not attractive will not help the process. Please note that this is the *only* time I advocate dishonesty in a relationship. Even still, you can be vague by telling your partner that you want an opportunity to reconnect with the world and better yourself. It's technically true.

And if by some chance you want to be friends with someone who cheated on you, don't say, "I can't stay with a cheater." Instead, tell him you don't feel secure in a romantic relationship with him anymore and that it's not necessarily his fault (even though it is, and personally, I would not hesitate to make that point clear). Whatever you say, do not give any hint at reconciliation if that is not your intention. Make it known that this is a *breakup* and not a break. Phrases like "I need space" and "We should see other people" can insinuate taking a break and should be avoided.

Don't tell him you want to be friends. He won't believe you. If he asks to remain friends, don't seem too eager. Tell him you think it's possible after enough time apart for reflection, but only time will tell. Maintaining neutrality will get him working just as hard to salvage a friendship.

Finally, don't forget the etiquette rules. End the conversation only when he's ready, and save your sigh of relief until after you leave. Don't stifle his emotions, and don't make the mistake of thinking he cares how you feel at this point.

Breaking up with someone is hard – surprise! Still, it's never in your best interest to take the easy way out. No matter how much you've been hurt by that person, you probably cared about his feelings at one point. Try to take the high road, but stay safe in the process.

The rest of this segment is for those who have been dumped.

There is no expected level of resilience for dealing with a breakup. Some people can take everything in stride, while others take months, even years to recover from losing someone they love. They might react angrily to being dumped, or they could sob uncontrollably. We all have different methods for grieving.

I listed the typical criteria for a clean breakup, but your "dumper" might not be so understanding and sensitive to your feelings. In that case, here are a few tried and true guidelines for maintaining your self-respect after being dumped:

1. Stay away for a while – Don't be the desperate stalker. Don't beg for forgiveness or tell him you want to change. What's done is done, and you need the space just as much as he does.

2. No benefits – Some people agree to be friends with benefits with the hope that it will become what they once had. You aren't dating him anymore, but you somehow think this is your way back

in. There will be jealousy and conflict once he moves on, and you won't enjoy the realization that you've been used.

3. Avoid the rebound – Read the segment after this one, and you will learn why a rebound is not a good idea. Take some time for self-reflection. You have plenty of time to waste before your next date; enjoy it.

4. Don't interfere when he finds someone new – It's not your place, and branding yourself as the jealous ex will only hinder your ability to attract someone new.

5. Make a list of all the things that are great about you – I'm just kidding; that's stupid. I saw it in an advice column about coping after a breakup and thought it was funny. Honestly, you don't need to write down your admirable qualities; you need to flaunt them.

6. The past is gone – Give his stuff back. Get rid of his e-mails and letters. Clean your living space of his presence, whether you want to use crystals and salt or just throw his shit away. If you keep this stuff for sentimental reasons, it appears as though you are not ready to move on. Your new partner will appreciate your lack of ex-boyfriendness in your bedroom.

Oh, and here's a good one: A girl told me one time that she was keeping her new boyfriend a secret out of respect for her ex. Meaning, she and this new guy were fully an official couple, engaging in all typical couple activities – but they had not made it public.

I know I'm preaching to well-informed adults here, but please don't do this. By having a private relationship, you are not respecting your ex; you are insulting his intelligence. What you do with your life is your business, but assuming that others care what you do with your life is presumptuous. Keeping your rebound a secret is worse than having a rebound in the first place.

In conclusion, I'm sorry about the breakup. Don't make it worse.

## *Your Rebound Is Not Different*

BETWEEN NOVEMBER and December every year – when seasonal affective disorder starts to set in – I get tons of letters about breaking up. Some of these breakups meant the end of what seemed like a solid relationship, while others were obvious inevitabilities. And the end of each letter begged the question: What's next?

In many cases, it's the infamous rebound – the failure of one relationship, the quick start of a new one, and the resolution to make this one work.

The rebound carries a negative connotation with almost everyone. The rebound is the temporary void-filler, the girl or guy who was "there for you, emotionally" when the nasty breakup happened. It's the person you knew you wanted all along but couldn't pursue because you were tied down. Oh, the poor rebound – doomed to be hurt from the beginning.

It's mostly true. While I know people who ended up marrying their rebounds, that's not normally what happens. You know that. But some refuse to agree and come to terms with what a rebound really is. They ignore the pain of the last breakup, deny the jealousy, and insist that they are only interested in moving forward. So, let's look at why people do it in the first place:

1. It shortens the grieving process – People who have been hurt tend to easily embrace a beautiful distraction such as a new romantic interest. This helps to suppress the initial pain – for a while, at least.

2. Dependency – Some people are dependent on constant companionship and hardly know what it's like to be alone, which is the problem: Being single is often associated with being alone.

3. Peer pressure – Observing others in seemingly happy relationships will drive you to be a part of that happiness again, doing whatever it takes.

4. Jealousy – Either because your ex has rebounded before you, or you want to rebound before your ex; it becomes a self-manufactured competition to make your ex jealous.

Those are the primary reasons, and rebounders who read this are no doubt shaking their heads and trying desperately to justify their exclusion from the above reasons. It's mostly true what they say about rebounds, you might tell me, but in the same breath you'll say your rebound is different – because he or she just happened to come around right at the time your past relationship was ending. So, that makes it fate. Ha.

When the breakup with a rebound happens, on comes a new wave of excuses and justifications. They blame the rebound for screwing something up, or they argue that the connection just kind of died. What they will continue to reiterate, though, is that the breakup had absolutely *nothing* to do with lingering feelings for their ex. That's fine. You can say that, but a rebound is still a rebound; and rebounds usually end.

Let's look at why rebound relationships eventually take a dive:

1. You successfully get over the pain from your last breakup. Subsequently, you realize you can do better than your rebound because you have finally regained your confidence.

2. You don't get over your ex, and you start to let it show by constantly talking about him or her. Instant breakup. Essentially, this is a rebound that ended prematurely.

3. The rebound does something to screw up the relationship. After all, rebounds aren't always the pick of the litter when it comes to dating material.

4. You do something to screw it up, likely the same thing you did to screw up the last relationship. You did not take enough time to reflect on your mistakes.

5. The relationship ends mutually when the initial spark of romance dies.

And that covers about ninety percent of all rebounds. I say ninety percent because I acknowledge the exceptions, and I realize that not every breakup is necessarily a painful one. Mutual breakups and other breakups that are generally easy can present opportunities for immediate prospects. But the success of any rebound is so rare that it's hardly worth mentioning.

For those who've recently become single and have considered dating again, don't think of this as a lashing. I don't want to discourage you from taking a chance with anyone you feel is worthy of your time. My advice about rebounding mainly goes out to my readers who have just left a long-term relationship: Even if you feel you're ready to hit the dating scene, take two months off instead. That's two months off from dating and interacting with anyone who could even remotely be considered a potential mate. This is your learning time. This is your opportunity to refine your observational skills.

Why two months? Because over the years of making mistakes, I've learned that it takes exactly one month before fully understanding what went wrong. Of course, some people need much more time to grieve and reflect, but I only speak to those who don't want to take any time at all.

If you were dumped, take a month to figure out why. If your ex did something to hurt you, take a month to figure out the telltale signs of a bad mate. It's not something you have to spend hours a day thinking about. I've found that it usually comes in the form of an epiphany. You might be in the shower, or just drifting off to sleep – or maybe you're sitting on the toilet doing a crossword puzzle. But it takes time to accept your flaws and your errors in judgment.

And the second month should be treated as buffer time to exercise your patience and figure out what you will do differently next time. If you can handle this, you have a real chance of getting somewhere with your next relationship. And it's not considered a rebound if you've waited long enough.

On the other hand, if after those two months you decide you don't have to recognize your faults, you'll want to try again after two or three more failed relationships.

## *Photo Revenge*

IN A TIME where the Internet has nearly prevailed over real life – and the Internet most certainly decides what the public should care about – it was only a matter of time before I received a letter like this one:

*Dear Stephen,*

*I guess this is what I get for dating a guy who spends his life online. I recently broke up with a*

129

*guy I had been dating for five months. It wasn't really a serious thing, and I figured there was no harm done. While we were together, I took erotic photos for him and e-mailed them to him, obviously for HIS EYES ONLY (and I told him this, of course). Well, the breakup pissed him off, and now my photos are on some public Internet message board, and now people from different parts of the world have seen me naked. This makes me seem like a total slut, which I'm not. How do I get my reputation back?*

*- Exposed*

Not a remarkable letter by any means, but an important one for this era. In the early '90s it was difficult for anyone to get this kind of exposure without some serious hard work. But this poor girl's ex-boyfriend barely had to lift his finger. There are quite a few message boards with world-wide fame, many of which have hundreds of thousands or even more than a million members. With that kind of easy access to such a large audience, one would think that a public posting of nude photos on the Internet could be the ultimate in embarrassment.

My reasoning, however, is that it's not nearly as bad as having those same pictures photocopied and posted around your own campus or workplace. The Internet audience surpasses a billion people, the vast majority of whom really don't care about you or what you look like naked – unless, of course, you are famous.

We live in the age of celebrity sex tapes and unintentionally (and intentionally) leaked nude pictures. For some, it's a career boost (See Paris Hilton and others), but then there are the somewhat damaging exposures such as the provocative photos of Disney Channel movie star Vanessa Hudgens that magically appeared on the Internet in September 2007. But the woman who wrote to me probably isn't auditioning for a part in a children's movie anytime soon. This was my response to her letter:

Dear Exposed,

If a celebrity has ever taken off his or her clothes in front of a camera, you can guarantee it's on the Internet. Most of us will roll our eyes and say, "Well, that's her fault for posing nude in front of a camera!"

Sucks when it happens to you, though.

You voluntarily took photos of your nude body and e-mailed them. This is what Disney Channel calls "a lapse in judgment." However, now that it has happened, there are maybe a few things you can do.

Your first option is to ignore it. You're not the first girl to be a victim of such a bastardly act. Taking erotic photos does not make you a slut; couples do this, and because of the seemingly limitless resources we have on the Internet these days, it has become the norm for private material to leak onto the Web. Why do you think intellectual property is so hard to protect nowadays? As you read this, there are at least half a dozen guys skimming through this article hoping to find a URL to your photos. And most of them wouldn't hesitate to share the photos with their buddies either.

Count yourself lucky that you aren't a celebrity. You are merely the victim of a boy seeking acceptance from his Internet buddies.

Just envision the message board post he made as such:

"Hay guyz mah gf broke up w/ me and i was mad cuz it shrunk my penis so now i'm gonna make my e-penis bigger by violating her trust and posting this nude pic LOLOL!

Here it is:

http://img133.imageshack.us/img133/5169/nudegfrk8.jpg

NSFW!!11"

While I don't mean to trivialize your situation, it's not always the best idea to bring attention to something that probably won't go further than a bunch of horny geeks you'll never meet. Yes, it's an invasion of your privacy and a horrible thing for him to do, but now you should just move on. He did it because he needed to make himself feel better, and now it's done. I don't think your photos will wind up on Perez-Hilton.com anytime soon.

But I will acknowledge that this is the best-case scenario. If you happen to be a public figure, or if you strongly feel that you're on your way to becoming one, this incident might be more damaging than it seems. Additionally, you never specified whether people you know have seen these pictures.

If there are factors that force you to be worried about your local reputation, here's another option: Take his ass to court.

I wish I knew about the law enough to say with certainty that you have a case, but from my understanding of copyright laws, it seems that because you took the photos, you own the copyrights to them. I also believe that if a photograph is taken with a digital camera, the copyright exists right at the time the image is saved anywhere, and as long as the photo exists in tangible form or can be reproduced with the aid of a machine, it is copyrighted. If this is the case, and if there are no inhibiting factors, you could sue him for copyright infringement.

If I'm wrong about this, perhaps you could take him to court for harassment or violation of privacy.

I know there is someone reading this who is an authority on the subject, and I invite you to e-mail me a clarification of these laws and a summary of what, if any, legal action can be taken.

Overall, my advice is to ignore it if it's humanly possible. And if you ever again decide to send your boyfriend nude photos, make sure he signs a privacy agreement, and have it notarized.

In other words, just don't do it.

No one ever clarified the legal aspect for me, but I did get a few more letters from women who wanted to offer suggestions for getting revenge. One of them explained how she started a nasty rumor about her ex-boyfriend's penis size after he showed his friends some compromising photos of her. But she makes sure to clarify that this all happened in high school and it's "just a suggestion." Another letter suggested I tell the girl to turn it into a positive thing and be proud of her body. Not a horrible idea, but I doubt even the proudest bodies in the world are proud to be stripped naked and shown to the public without permission.

If you ever end up in a situation where an ex has taken revenge on you by invading your privacy, counter-revenge isn't the answer for an obvious reason: If you one-up him, he'll just get more creative. I don't think being proud or further bringing attention to it is such a great idea either.

Many of us have been the subject of nasty rumors and secrets made public, and I've learned that the best thing to do is let it lie. The people who will remain important in your life are smart enough to understand the psychology of the situation. Pity the exes who have taken such measures for self-reassurance. They've rendered themselves too risky to date.

## The Relationship Bandwagon

I WANT to end this part of the book with one final, short note about relationships: You don't have to be in one right now.

College is the opportunity to get out of your comfort zone and meet people in other fields of interest, which can lead to a fulfilling long-term relationship; however, a good romance is never the result of unwanted pressure.

Just as I tell people not to sit around and wait for a relationship to fall in their laps, I don't advocate forcing a bond that isn't there. There is no reason you can't stay single throughout your college years. Just be open to whatever comes your way, and if you aren't ready to jump on the first relationship bandwagon, there will be a next one. The first one, however, will not circle the block for you.

# 6

# Selections

As much as I'd like it to be, this book is not an all-inclusive guide. My goal has been to provide readers with the most important issues of being in love and in college, but some topics need to be experienced rather than discussed. And some topics don't warrant their own sections, which is why I feel this chapter is necessary to fill in a few cracks.

I've compiled twenty questions and answers that I feel would be of some use to you, though they don't quite fit in with any of the other topics – or at least I couldn't figure out how to fit them. If you're interested in topics about suicidal exes, masturbation, threesomes, getting ditched for friends, low self-esteem, and more, enjoy these quickies.

### Should I Marry My Pregnant Girlfriend?

$Q1$: "I got my girlfriend pregnant, and now her parents are saying I should either marry her or stay out of her life. She's moved to the next town over to live with her family. My parents say I should not marry her, but I want to do the right thing. Which is best for the child?"

Answer: Both of you are adults. More importantly, both of you are about to be parents. Given that, anything your mommies and daddies say is merely an opinion. And it's an opinion that hardly matters, to be honest.

The minute you received the news that you were going to be a father, your priorities were taken from you, shuffled, re-ordered, and given back to you in the form of a flashing neon sign. Your baby is now more important than your own life.

Your existence on this earth has become about the child and how both of you will take care of it. Guess who becomes irrelevant? Ding ding ding! The parents! Acknowledge their wishes, and respectfully decline.

Don't marry this girl if there is any shred of doubt (which there is) in your mind that it will be a successful marriage. Either way, you still have a right to see your child. Sure, she can make that difficult for you by moving away and staying close to her parents – but her parents can't force her to do this. She's making the decision to put her family's wishes above the best interest of the baby. This makes her a bad parent from the start.

You need to remind her of her adulthood and that she is ultimately in charge of her own decisions. Both of you need to work together – emotionally, physically, and financially – to provide a real home for this child, married or not. You two can worry about yourselves later, because you simply aren't that important right now.

### Why Is He Ditching Me For His Friends?

**Q2**: "My boyfriend and I had plans a week in advance to go to a club with a group of my friends. The night we were supposed to go, he calls me at work and tells me that he all of a sudden did not like the club and did not feel like going. I still went with my friends.

"However, I found out that my boyfriend actually stayed up all night playing video games with his friends that night. No big deal, except that this was the only day I would've been able to see him that week, and he knew that. Not only that, but he spent three other days with his friends that week, too.

"Now, I know my boyfriend is going camping this weekend with his friends, so I would like to spend some time with him when he comes back. Yet again, his friends have plans to get together during the weekday and get drunk at a camp. Yes, I was invited, but I do not plan on missing anymore school, so I decided to decline.

"I've had bad experiences with people and alcohol earlier in life. My boyfriend and I promised to never drink without each other, and this was his idea. But again, he's favoring his friends' suggestion. I feel like he is constantly doing this. When I bring it up, all he does is try to make me feel guilty. Is there *any* way to approach this situation right? I just want to be able to see him more often."

**Answer**: He apparently doesn't have his priorities in order, and he's putting his friends over you more often than a boyfriend should. But here's the big question: How often is too often?

This depends on the type of relationship you and he share. Juggling friends and romance can be tricky business when the two can't be mixed. And it sounds like his relationship with his friends and his relationship with you are being kept separate, either by you or by him.

Sometimes, men can get carried away and lose track of their social priorities. Many of us feel more comfortable with our male friends than we do with the girlfriend, simply because of society's standards. We have to act differently around women, more so with the girlfriend than with our female friends. No matter what a woman might say or do to alleviate that requirement, there's still our subconscious that sometimes makes us feel trapped into being someone we're not.

If you get to the point where you don't appreciate the time you do spend together and instead harp on the times he favors his friends over you, the whole thing will become too mentally exhausting for him to handle. And like anyone, he will start to always choose what's easier for him: his friends. I'm sure he had a lot of fun with his friends; he had enough fun to justify the fact that he'd later have to deal with a very upset girlfriend.

Both of you have to come to an agreement on whether the idea of keeping friends and romance separate is going to work. If he invites you to hang out with his friends and you keep saying no, he will stop inviting you. There's nothing you can do about that.

The best thing you can do at this point is try to reach a compromise that fulfills your emotional and physical needs in the relationship, but at the same time, gives your boyfriend enough breathing room to still have as much fun with his friends as he does with you.

On that note, you should think about how you two interact when you're alone – be aware of any judgment you cast or personal conduct standards that prevent him from acting natural around you. You are not expected to be "one of the guys," but you do need to be a friend.

It was a bad idea for him to ever make an agreement with you about drinking, no matter who initiated it. Drinking can be a big deal to some people, but it's also a small obstacle that friends and couples overcome with a little bit of maturity and reasoning.

However, because he made the promise, he needs to do a whole lot more than say, "Hey, my friends want me to drink with them, so forget the promise." He invited you to drink at the camp, so he feels that you declining the invite does not nullify his freedom to drink. But if this is not OK with you, tell him; just be prepared to intelligently defend your objection.

Relationships are about compromise and acceptance, but they are *not* about excessive self-sacrifice of either person's freedom to be genuine. And if that's what this relationship requires from either of you, then it's not going to work. That's life, and you're still young.

Best of luck to you, "Feeling Neglected."

### My Ex Threatened Suicide – What Do I Do?

$Q3$: "I dated this guy for about five months, which is actually my longest relationship yet. I'm not really ready to do anything serious, and even though I think he's a really great guy, I told him I was ready to move on and see other people. I didn't want him out of my life or anything, because who knows? Maybe we could get back together later or something.

"I called him last night, and when I told him this, he got really upset. He told me he loved me and he couldn't live without me, and that if I really wanted him gone he would end his life right now, and he hung up. I was too shaken to do anything, but I know he didn't do it because I saw him on campus today. I am really scared for him because he's never seemed like the kind of guy who would be so depressive and, well, emo. I don't want to be responsible for driving some guy to suicide! I really hope you can help."

**Answer:** It doesn't take an expert to spot an obvious cry for attention. "Emo" people don't necessarily have to look the part all the time. What you're dealing with is immaturity on an unfathomable scale. Hide the razors, or else he might need a Band-Aid or two.

But all joking aside, you still have a semi-serious problem here. He probably won't kill himself, but this guy is a potential stalker. If his reaction to ending such a short relationship was so grim, there's a possibility that the madness won't stop there.

The best thing for you to do at this point is teach him a lesson about crying for attention with such a serious claim. He talked about killing himself, so now you're obligated to do something about it. Call his parents and friends. Make sure everyone who cares about him knows what he told you. After all, you're trying to help him. And when his friends and family are all over him, see if he ever says something like that again.

**Where Are The Guys Who Want My Personality?**

**Q4**: "I have never had a boyfriend, ever. I know it's because I'm overweight and definitely not as attractive as most of the girls here, but now I am starting to feel lonely, as it seems like it's all about looks and not personality. I know not everyone judges on looks alone, but it seems like I fall for the ones who say they only like me as a friend or like someone else. How do I find the guy who will give me a chance?"

**Answer:** You're right about two things: (1) It's all about looks, and (2) Not everyone judges on looks alone. Sounds paradoxical, eh? Well, yep.

We're human, and we can't help but notice the most attractive person in the room. And yes, the more confident of us choose that person as the target of our lust. Guys are going to hit on the hot girl.

But you know what? That's life, and that doesn't mean the rest of us have to live in solitude. Whether or not the hot girl is a cliché dimwit is irrelevant. The point is, you aren't a super model, so you can't expect to jump on the relationship boat without getting your feet wet.

My advice to you is to mentally, physically, and emotionally be in a place where you are comfortable with yourself. Confidence and happiness are the biggest factors in finding a real mate, and if you are confident with the way you look and feel, or if you are a happy person in general, you won't have a hard time finding men who want to be a part of your intellectual stability. To me, that's the hottest thing ever.

## Do I Have Time For A Boyfriend?

$Q5$: "My brain is getting fried from school. I'm loaded down, in over my head. I'm graduating in May, but in order to do that I had to get special permission to take twenty-one hours. On top of that, I have to wait tables at night. One big problem is my boyfriend. He doesn't go to my school, so we don't get to see each other often. Now I'm afraid it's going to be even less. On top of school and work are other responsibilities, and I feel like I just need to get rid of something. But what? Do I even have time for a boyfriend?"

Answer: I would look at this semester as your sprint to the finish. You're out of there in less than four months, and this is the final test – the epitome of what you've endured for almost four years or even longer. You probably need the job to pay bills, and your other responsibilities are exactly that: responsibilities.

But that's not a fun way of looking at it. It certainly doesn't help you enjoy anything more by telling yourself you're obligated to do it.

My advice to you – and it's something I try to do – is to look for opportunities to reward yourself for trudging through your daily responsibilities. I'm not talking about big rewards like going out and getting smashed just for reading a chapter in your textbook. Do small things to relax your mind, like watching your favorite TV show after studying for an hour or two.

Now, granted, you could just disobey yourself and watch it anyway, but the key is to force yourself to stay on track, so when the reward comes, it's all the more satisfying if you deserved it.

And to conclude my thoughts, here's one last important thing: There is no such thing as not having time for a boyfriend or girlfriend, but there is such a thing as not having time for an unreasonable one. Don't get rid of the wrong things.

### Why Do I Dump Them After A Few Months?

$Q6$: "It seems that with every guy I date, I start losing interest after a few months and dump him. This has probably happened about four times. It will be fun for the first three months, and then I'll wait another month until I'm just bored to tears. Now it's happening with my current boyfriend. We've been together for nine months, which is my longest relationship ever, and it's happening again! What's wrong with me?"

Answer: What you have is a mild case of normal. You're young and still have a lot of living to do. Naturally, dating is going to play a big role in this "living" you're doing. It all goes with the college experience. However, if you're finding this unrelenting streak of boredom to be a problem, read on.

Starting a new relationship is great. In fact, most people agree that the first two weeks or so are going to be the best moments of the relationship (the first few months of marriage being the exception). This is not to give you a pessimistic outlook; it's merely to help you understand that even the best things in life can become dull once you've experienced them enough.

In the typical happy cookie-cutter boy-meets-girl experience, girl and boy like each other, girl and boy go out on a date, girl and boy still like each other, girl and boy change their respective Facebook relationship statuses.

Boy and girl then become well-acquainted with one another. Boy and girl have deep, fascinating conversations, wild sex, and a common bond of knowing everything about each other.

Then, boy and girl are done with the bulk of the learning. The sex is fairly predictable. And alas, boy and girl get bored sometimes.

So, what do you do with your brand new car after you figure out all the nifty features on it? You drive it. What do you do with your new computer after you install all your software and learn how to use it? Well, you use it.

And what do you do when you get a new significant other and learn all of his personality quirks and hear tales of his exciting past, present, and future? You decide whether or not you like everything you know about him – and if so, you live your lives together.

When you make that decision, you might feel as if you're faced with another dilemma: Does having a long-term boyfriend inhibit my full college experience?

Dating does not have to make social hermits of us all, but the bottom line is that it's up to you. You can decide you want to experience the dating world a little more before settling, or you can keep my thoughts in mind the next time you're feeling bored. There is no right or wrong answer – only results.

### How Do I Help Him Get Over His Stress?

**Q7:** "My boyfriend tends to get sidetracked and become stressed. For the past month or two, he has been working over thirty hours a week and doing studies/homework the night or three hours before his class.

"His stress has caused him to be sick sometimes, and worst of all, overreact. He believes that he will lose me if he does not succeed in everything that he does. I will not leave him, and it is hard to convince him. I am doing my best to help him, but what else is there for me to do?"

**Answer**: It happens to the best of us. The stress certainly isn't helping him, but he may have a slight chemical imbalance. It's not necessarily caused by the fact that he's so busy all the time, but working thirty hours a week and going to school is preventing him from being able to take a breather and reevaluate.

In my opinion, he doesn't really believe he will lose you if he doesn't succeed. It seems like a way for him to seek attention from the best source of all, his girlfriend. Every time he tells you that, he's simply looking for the same reassurance.

This does not mean he will simply accept what you're saying and move on. His amount of stress (and maybe depression) causes him to think irrationally. While he is subconsciously fulfilled by your constant reassurance, he argues outwardly. This is because a stressed person can do nothing better than create even more stress for himself.

Help him make observations on his lifestyle. How well is he managing the precious time he has every day? How much sleep is he getting, and how much potential sleep is he missing as a result of bad time management? Perhaps you could help him figure out where he can cut back on his workload. You can even go as far as helping him make a budget to figure out if he really needs to be working so many hours.

Cutting back on responsibilities is not always possible, but it's worth a shot. The key to helping him evaluate his workload and

Selections

time management is to be more passive than critical. Overall, your job as the girlfriend is to counteract his stress in any way you can. It may not seem like it, but he probably appreciates everything you do for him.

### How Do I Tell My Friend I Don't Like Her New Guy?

**Q8**: "I'll just come right out and say it: My best friend's new boyfriend is an asshole. He is a worthless loser, and he is not worthy of her or anyone else in this world for that matter. He treats her like crap, doesn't have a job, makes her pay for everything, is verbally abusive, and they have nothing in common. There are so many things I want to tell her about this piece of shit, but I need to know how to word it perfectly."

**Answer**: There are two things you need to realize: First, you are obligated to tell her that you disapprove of her boyfriend. Second, she will not listen to you.

Your friend inevitably suffers from New Relationship Syndrome (NRS) right now, and nothing you say will help her see anything different about him. But grit your teeth and tell her how you feel, and try to bear through the excuses she'll be spewing at you. Here's my favorite: "He's different when we're alone."

You have to go through the motions of warning her about him, because you're a bad friend if you don't. Eventually, she'll wise up and see everything you see. If you kept your observations to yourself the whole time, you will get blamed for her suffering. But don't be angry at your friend for thoughtlessly ignoring you; a nasty case of NRS might be in store for you one day, too, or maybe

147

you've already experienced it. If you believe her safety is at risk, however, take action immediately.

### Should Guys Be Calling My Girlfriend This Much?

**Q9**: "My girlfriend is a bartender, and there have been a few times where male customers made advances toward her and she did not stand up for our relationship. She just laughed and went on.

"We broke up for twenty-one days, and she gave her phone number out to a few interested guys. We are back together now. Is it appropriate for these guys to call her now? She still sees them at work. They call her and say stuff like, 'Hi, sweetie. What are you bringing us for lunch?' and so on. One time, she said, 'I'm with my boyfriend,' and the guy said, 'What?…Oh, he's right next to you?' Do I have a right to be upset about all this?"

**Answer**: Beginning with your first problem, I want to remind you – in case you forgot – that you are dating a bartender. Guys will hit on her; they will ask her for her number; they will ask her what she's doing after work.

It's the nature of the job, and her reaction to these advances determines how large her tip will be. She's not cheating on you in that sense; she's merely responding appropriately so she can come home with more than just the satisfaction of an honest day's work.

I hope you didn't allow the relationship to end for this reason. But if you did, what were you expecting the second time around?

I don't think it will be a problem for you to accept the social requirements of her job as a bartender, but these "gentleman callers" are a different animal. It is not part of her job.

When you and your girlfriend weren't together, she had every right to accumulate dating prospects. But if you're in an exclusive relationship, and both of you understand that it's exclusive, these other men should stay behind the solid red line surrounding you and your girlfriend.

When men call her for what seems like the sole reason of flirting, it's breaking common relationship rules and boundaries, and what's worse is that your girlfriend isn't stopping it. It's fine for her to have male friends, but as soon as they cross the line, it's up to her to put her foot down and give fair warning.

"Oh, he's right next to you?" – this might sound like she could be cheating, but to give her a little credit, I'd say the guy is just trying to rile you up and put you on edge. You're letting him do it; but then again, so is she.

I don't know either of you, but from your letter, it still seems to me that instead of respecting you and the relationship by setting boundaries with these men, your girlfriend is basking in the attention. This is her personality; decide whether it's manageable, and take it from there.

### Is His Dog More Important Than Me?

$Q10$: "My boyfriend recently introduced me to his dog. This was planned for weeks; seriously. He wanted to 'prepare' his dog to meet me, and he said it is very important that I make a good first impression…on his dog. HIS DOG!

"The meeting went fine. It sniffed my hand and licked it a little bit. He made me shake hands with it. It's a nice dog and everything, but now that we've 'met,' my boyfriend insists on bringing the dog everywhere. Even on date nights at my apartment, he brings the dog. He treats it like a human, and he seems to value its opinion of me. It's kind of freaking me out. The dog is getting in the way of us having a normal intimate relationship. I've been with this guy for two months now. Other than this, everything is fine. But what have I gotten into?"

**Answer**: I've always felt that dogs are more intuitive than humans when it comes to figuring out the intentions of other animals. I also believe that dogs, as well as many other animals, can see things we can't see – if such things exist. Additionally, I know that animals are rightfully very important to most people, and it can hurt a relationship if a couple sharply disagrees on pet issues.

Having said that, however, this is nuts.

It shouldn't be difficult to look past his obsession about the dog's opinion of you – that's over and done. The dog likes you.

But, in my opinion, there are only three reasons he should be bringing the dog with him on what are supposed to be intimate dates: (1) The dog is new and needs more care and attention the first few weeks in his new home, (2) It is sick or injured and needs to be monitored, or (3) There is a circumstance where the dog is not safe or should not be home at the moment.

Other than that, Daddy and his new girlfriend need private time.

He's obviously attached to his trusted companion, so don't expect him to stop bringing the dog to your apartment. It's not your job to break him of this; he has to learn on his own that it's a problem, or he has to find someone who accepts it. Still, you can ask for compromise. When he brings the dog over, try to make a temporary place for it to be safe and secure – and barricaded – in your apartment. If the dog has a nasty habit of sneaking up on you mid-coitus, there is no reason it should be allowed to roam free during that time. The last thing a caring boyfriend would want is for you to resent him or anything he values.

If, on the other hand, your boyfriend enjoys the extra company in bed, good luck with that one.

### How Do I Deal With His Low Self-Esteem?

$Q11$: "My new boyfriend constantly puts himself down about everything. He thinks he's horrible at kissing, dancing, sex, talking, etc. I try to tell him it's not true, but he continues to ramble on about how he doesn't feel adequate. It was cute at first, but it's really starting to annoy me. How do I get it through to him that I appreciate everything about him?"

**Answer**: There comes a point where you must decide if dealing with low self-esteem issues is feasible for you. Depending on his level of insecurity, it can get rougher as the relationship becomes more serious. I know a girl who would literally vomit every time her boyfriend gave her a compliment or tried to get intimate. It proved to be too difficult to handle, and they drifted apart.

Your situation seems milder, though it should not be taken lightly. Others might say he's looking for a little reassurance and some compliments, but it could very well be a newly acquired character trait – a habit that will be hard to break.

Another talk is in order, and this one should be about *your* needs in the relationship. Make it clear to your boyfriend that if there's something bothersome about him, you won't hesitate to bring it to his attention. You should not be solely responsible for moving this relationship forward. If he doesn't understand this, you shouldn't waste your time on something that will inevitably become too much for you to bear.

You can make it a priority to talk to him about his feeling of self-worth regularly and even encourage him to get help in a support group (which you should attend, too). Above all, you should continue to remind your boyfriend about the beauty of being human.

### Why Is She Surprised That I Masturbate?

**Q12**: "My girlfriend and I had the masturbation talk a while back, and she was actually shocked to learn that I masturbate. I told her that a man has needs, and since she and I only have sex once a week, I sometimes do it to relieve stress. Is that wrong?"

**Answer**: As hard as it is to believe, some people just don't masturbate. If your girlfriend is one of those who believe masturbation is only for single, sexually inactive people, there's not much you can do to sway her to the dark side.

You have every right to satisfy yourself, as long as it doesn't interfere with your relationship and sex life (i.e. the real stuff). It's not cheating unless you're crossing preset boundaries. But much like the topic of pooping, it's not really worth discussing with your partner in detail.

### How Do I Trust Men Again?

**Q13**: "I ended a long-term relationship and found out the guy cheated on me with a close friend. I'm starting to feel like I can't trust men anymore, as this is not the first time something similar has happened to me. Is there anything I can do to help myself build that trust again?"

**Answer**: You know better than that; however, I understand your hesitance to trust another man anytime soon. Just realize that even though you don't deserve what has happened to you, there might be a trend in the type of men you choose to date.

I won't tell you to try dating someone completely different from your usual pick, but perhaps this time you should explain yourself before things get too serious. Tell your new boyfriend you've been hurt in the past. While he should not have to pay for your past boyfriends' mistakes, you would do well to ask him for a little patience and guidance to show you that not all men are cheaters and liars.

### Should I Sleep With My Best Friend?

**Q14**: "I've known my best friend for almost ten years. I'm female and he's male. He's a very nice guy, and we get along for the most part. I am very comfortable with him, and we have joked about the idea of having sex. I know he is serious, and I am not sure how I feel. Would having sex ruin the friendship? Or should we date before pursuing sexual intimacy?"

**Answer**: You might know each other quite well, but you should not ignore the fact that you have not been sexually intimate together – it will change things. He will have new expectations from the friendship, and he might even wish to take things further than you ever intended.

Sex for pleasure is fine, but with such a life-long friend, you run the risk of damaging the preexisting bond. There might not be permanent damage, but I can almost guarantee it will be a different experience than what you've envisioned.

If you aren't sure about it, and he seems more serious than you'd like, I recommend leaving the situation alone for now until you've made a firm decision about dating him. If you think it's possible to start a relationship with him, you'd be a fool not to try; but if you think you can establish a strictly physical relationship with a guy – a good friend – who you've known for a decade, you're only fooling yourself.

### Am I Too Paranoid About Being Raped?

**Q15**: "I have been sexually active since college. However, I have an unrelenting fear of being raped. I worry when I go out late at night, when I walk to my car in the dark, and sometimes I have un-founded fears that the guy I'm dating will attempt to rape me. Am I being paranoid?"

**Answer**: With genuine and shocking rape statistics being thrown every which way these days, it's not even about paranoia anymore; it's about being cautious. But don't let it get in the way of having a practical relationship.

Travel on foot in groups, never leave your drink unattended, and carry something with you for self-defense. There are plenty of resources on the Internet that can help you protect yourself against

Selections

rape and tell you what to do if it happens. It's important to be cautious; just don't lose any sleep over it.

### I'm A Girl Who Loves Sex. So What?

**Q16**: "I know the general idea is that guys love sex. But I am a girl, and I enjoy having sex all the time. Sex does not have to be emotional for me, and sometimes it is just easier to be pleasured without having the attachment to another person. How do I get others to stop judging me? Guys are not judged for having sex without emotion. Should I just lie and keep it a secret?"

**Answer**: Unfortunately, I can't single-handedly abolish the double standard. Your actions will always be under scrutiny by those around you.

You will be judged for having sex. You will be judged for not having sex. You will be judged for keeping your sex life a secret, and you'll be judged for making it public. Do what makes you feel comfortable, paying little attention to what others think. Stay safe, and be smart about it. But in every sense of the phrase, fuck 'em.

### If We Have A Threesome, Will He Cheat?

**Q17**: "My boyfriend and I have been together about a year. We mutually decided to try a threesome. But, now that we talk about it a lot, I am worried he will start cheating on me. Is that a valid fear?"

**Answer**: Yes, it's a valid fear. Before you go any further, you will have to set some very specific, loophole-free ground rules. Not for his sake, but for yours. If you're having doubts about trying a ménage à trois, I recommend waiting, but the rules will at least help prevent something unexpected from happening. For help on setting some safe boundaries, visit www.askmen.com and search "threesome rules."

### Why Does She Want Me To Help Plan The Wedding?

**Q18**: "I recently got engaged, and my fiancée is running me ragged with wedding plans. She wants me to be a part of every decision regarding the ceremony, the reception, the music, the food, the color scheme, etc.

"She won't accept 'I don't care,' even though I really *don't* care. It should be the bride's decision for the most part. How do I get her to quit asking for my opinion, which never seems to be on the same page as hers?"

**Answer**: The wedding is technically for both of you. In practical terms, however, it's her wedding. This means you get to voice your suggestions, and she gets to deny them. Humor her with your baseless opinions, and when she disagrees, emphasize how right she is. Be a sincere, kind, caring, valuable yes-man.

### How Do I Forgive Such Betrayal?

**Q19**: "My best friend slept with my boyfriend. I know friends last longer than boyfriends, but how do I let go of my boyfriend and forgive my friend?"

**Answer**: You can dump them both. Just because she's a friend doesn't mean she has amnesty from pissing you off. What she did is a big deal; you have no obligation to remain close friends with her if you don't want to.

### Is Dating A Coworker A Good Idea?

**Q20**: "There's a guy at work who seems to like me, and I think I'm falling for him. But I know there's always a risk with dating coworkers. It can go sour, and things can get awkward, or one of us could get a promotion one day and cause conflict of interest. Any safe plays for this situation?"

**Answer**: There's almost always some level of risk associated with dating, and inter-office relationships throw just one more bit of danger into the mix. If you think you want to date this guy, don't cheat yourself out of a potential relationship based on the risk of workplace drama.

Before that first date, however, discuss a few details with him: Should it be kept a secret from the coworkers and bosses? Are you both prepared to continue working in the same environment if the relationship doesn't work out?

Also, many employers discourage dating coworkers, and some will even separate couples, either by rescheduling work hours or moving desks. If, as mature adults, both of you understand the rules and are willing to play by them, enjoy your date.

www.ingramcontent.com/pod-product-compliance
Lightning Source LLC
Chambersburg PA
CBHW030016290326
41934CB00005B/356